+0

[for other titles and publications please refer to end page]

A QUESTION FOR

Pope John Paul II

FROM JOHN METCALFE

A QUESTION FOR Pope John Paul II

FROM JOHN METCALFE

THE PUBLISHING TRUST

John Metcalfe Publishing Trust
Penn, Buckinghamshire

—

First published 1980

—

—

ISBN 0 9506366 4 9

—

Printed by M. & A. Thomson Litho Ltd.
East Kilbride
Cover by Studio ISP
High Wycombe

—

Price £1.25

J. M. P. T.

'And Jesus answered and said unto them,
I will also ask of you one question,
and answer me,
and I will tell you by what authority I do these things.'

Mark 11:29

THE AUTHOR

John Metcalfe is the son of a city magnate. His
father was a director of several household-
name companies, prominent in the booming
film industry, Gaumont and Odeon Cinemas,
later closely associated with Lord Rank; now
living in the South of France.

After four years at sea in the Merchant Navy,
John Metcalfe sailed on M.V. *Gambia Palm* to
the west coast of Africa; up river at Sapele he
was brought face to face with his Maker.
Returning to London, Metcalfe was remarkably
converted.

After serving with 'Youth for Christ' John
Metcalfe was called to the Congregational
Ministry. He became disillusioned with the
state of the church.

Consequently he sought God in solitude for
seven years of prayer, lonely vigil, and
painstaking study of the scripture.

Returning to the churches, John Metcalfe
became well known as an evangelist and
teacher with the Movement for World
Evangelisation.

Still burdened for a deeper, more far-reaching
repentance in both church and ministry than
yet experienced, Metcalfe returned for three
further years of solitary prayer and exacting
study.

Founding Tylers Green Chapel and the Trust,
as a direct consequence of his years apart the
present book is written in which he asks
questions and looks for answers from Pope
John Paul II.

A QUESTION FOR Pope John Paul II

FROM JOHN METCALFE

Sir,

No one will deny the tremendous appeal that has been felt all over the world in consequence of your recent journeys. The strength of your character, the impact of your personality, the moral tone of your discourses: all these are beyond question.

This is just as true of your transparent humility. Everything about you — your whole humanity — appears so evidently rooted in toil and in affinity with the poor of the earth, the tillage of the soil: no wonder you made such an impact!

None can deny — even if the brutish ignore — your uncompromising respect for the sanctity of life, of unborn life, of the right to live, of your unerring touch upon chords that resonate in the life of humanity, unbroken

1

from heart to heart, from age to age, to all generations. You have touched that humanity, and for a moment the world has listened. How rare!

Respecting the human decencies and — alas — conflicts and sufferings, no one can deny the things which you have said or the way that you have said them. You have spoken of the right to freedom and dignity, of the inherent liberties of man. Men everywhere have inclined their ear. For an instant the peoples have listened. The United Nations have been still whilst you have spoken.

These things being so, and moreover universally acclaimed as so — the world itself bearing witness — who is he that shall lift the voice of dissent? Or why? And about what? Who dare raise a complaint in the face of these triumphs? Shall any be found with the temerity to protest?

Certainly not the heirs of Protestantism: bowing down with one accord beneath the spell of your charisma, their catholic spirit was evident and is evident. Neither yet the children of nonconformity: their conformity was demonstrable and is demonstrable.

Your visits, appearances and influence show that on every hand the world acknowledges the papal presence as radiating the aspirations of human endeavour and idealism. To many, perhaps even of survival. Covert or overt, the testimony of Christendom voices with unanimity the confession that the Roman Catholic church remains the bulwark and hope of an otherwise disintegrating Christianity.

Then who am I to lift up the voice?

for Pope John Paul II

As to this world, nothing. Less than nothing. Though born to some honour, what things were gain to me, these I lost, and, like the prodigal son in the parable, dissipated all that I had in the far country. I became what I am in truth: nothing. Less than nothing.

Then so high a dignitary as the Pope might well dismiss such a person — a nonentity, an upstart — entirely as beneath his notice. He might preserve an aloof and silent dignity, like that of the virtuous elder brother towards that wretched penitent, the prodigal son.

He might, Sir, but for two extenuating circumstances.

The first is, that a greater than the Pope has not disdained my cry, nor shut his ear to my utterance. For this poor man cried, and the LORD heard him and saved him out of all his troubles. Far above Italy or Poland, England or the world; beyond our generation, outside of time: the high and lofty One that inhabiteth eternity, whose name is Holy, who dwells with him that is of a humble and contrite heart, that trembleth at his word: He hath heard me.

Will not then the Pope?

God despises not the poor in spirit, yea, a broken and a contrite heart, O Lord, thou shalt not despise.

Then shall the Pope despise what God hath not disdained?

Since of God I have obtained mercy and gained audience, I find in this a cause, an extenuating circumstance, to address my question, Sir, to you also.

3

The next cause is this.

Twenty years of my life had passed before I made the least acquaintance with religion, the Bible, the church, or of anything to do with even the outward profession of Christianity. There was nothing in my home, background or years at sea. Nothing. Only after that time, broken and destitute, chastened, ready to die, then the love of the Father drew to his Son this lost wanderer, this poor outcast. He revealed his love to this miserable Jonah, who truly believed himself to have forfeited all love, to have gone beyond hope or reach even of human friendship.

That so lovely a Redeemer, so interior a Saviour, should love me and — wonderful revelation — reveal that love in me, within my broken heart: oh, overwhelming. Revelation in a glory so infinitely radiant and surpassing all compassion: oh, Sir, I cannot express. I am overcome to this day.

Should I not love much, when much is forgiven? Surely this gives some right to testify? For in the twenty-eight years since, I cannot but say that I am moved to love him more abundantly. Reminiscent of the light under which Saul was converted, Acts 9:3,

> 'Suddenly there shined round about him
> a light from heaven,'

the radiance brightens as the Day draws nearer. The apostle Paul recalls this thirteen chapters later, saying,

> 'Suddenly there shone from heaven
> a great light round about me.'

It had become great. It became greater to him as time

4

passed. So that finally, Acts 26:13, the apostle exclaims as he soars in triumph:

'At midday, O king,'

— nature's created light, though at the zenith, unequal to the task —

'I saw in the way
a light from heaven, above the brightness of the sun.'

How the glory increased in his experience, at last putting all nature to shame and darkness.

And whilst of course I saw no exterior light nor outward vision, yet I cannot deny seeing the inward glory, and beholding an interior inshining. Nor can I deny that this has increased to me more and more towards the perfect day.

'For God,
who commanded the light to shine out of darkness,
hath shined in our hearts,
to give the light of the knowledge of the glory of God
in the face of Jesus Christ.'

That is my experience, and blessed be God, these twenty-eight years past, it has increased in glory. From glory to glory, even as beholding the face of the LORD.

However, it is not this marvellous light shining in the heart, but rather what has appeared to me outwardly in the church during the same period, that moves me to write. It is in the contrast between these two, the difference between what the Lord reveals within and what the church appears without — during the same twenty-eight years — that I find what at last constrains me to take up my pen.

A Question

And I feel that here is a second extenuating circumstance that allows a person so insignificant as myself to ask your kind consideration of my question.

During this period, and over this conflict between what was within and without, I have gone to this man and that. This Catholic and that Protestant. This church, that assembly. This gathering, that meetinghouse. I have heard the evangelicals, the high churchmen. I have listened to the fundamentalists and the sacramentalists. I have given ear to the great preachers, old men now, or dead, who seemed to be pillars, evangelicals or otherwise. I have suffered the endless opinionated droning of a multitude of lesser brethren — but not in their own eyes — of truly meagre stature. All this time.

But now I feel that if I should hold my peace the very stones might cry out.

The old men, the old priests, the old doctors, the old ministers have come and gone. They have uttered what passed for wisdom. They have left behind their books, both old and new. This they have done, these dead men who have passed on, to show the living how to go.

But all this time I ached within myself. Like the prophet of old, I cried, My bowels, my bowels! For there was within me as a fire shut up. God knoweth my pain within me; and my tears are not hid from his sight.

But does this give me a right to speak? Is this an extenuating circumstance? Where is the precedent?

When Job was afflicted, when his soul passed through profound trials, when he cried for one that could understand or speak to his case, one of a thousand, an interpreter, one to speak from God, as out of heaven, then the old men came. Eliphaz and Bildad, they came. Zophar, he came. And, 'Miserable comforters are ye all.'

And so I found after twenty-eight years of seeing inwardly a glory in Christ, yet viewing outwardly a rent and divided sectarianism, a mockery of the church, content without that glory. Of hearing within the voice of the Son of God; and sounding without, the voice of contradictory man. And all this from those who were supposed to be the wise men. 'Miserable comforters are ye all.'

But is that in itself extenuating? An extenuating precedent for me to take it upon myself to speak?

'Now Elihu had waited till Job had spoken, because they were elder than he.

> 'I am young,
> and ye are very old;
> wherefore I was afraid,
> and durst not show you mine opinion.

> I said,
> Days should speak,
> and multitude of years should teach wisdom.

> But there is a spirit in man:
> and the inspiration of the Almighty
> giveth them understanding.

> Behold,
> I waited for your words;
> I gave ear to your reasons, whilst ye searched out what to say.

'They were amazed; they answered no more; they left off speaking.

A Question

'I said,
I will answer also my part,
I also will show mine opinion.

For I am full of matter,
the spirit within me constraineth me.

Behold, my belly is as wine which hath no vent;
it is ready to burst like new bottles.

I will speak, that I may be refreshed:
I will open my lips and answer.

Let me not, I pray you, accept any man's person,
neither let me give flattering titles unto man.

For I know not to give flattering titles;
in so doing my maker would soon take me away.'

Here, Sir, I find cause to speak to you, and for you to answer me. My cause and authority is this — Elihu having given precedent — that which David utters, and the apostle himself echoes:

'I believed: therefore I spake.'

By these two circumstances, by the twenty-eight years between them, I beg leave to be heard; for these are not light words, nor do they come from my mind as speculative. Here is the cry and voice of the heart; from the spirit they sound. 'Deep calleth unto deep at the noise of thy waterspouts.'

So much then for my taking it upon myself — who am nothing — to address my superior, who is altogether above my lowly place. If my reasons are wrong, let them be shown to be wrong. Then I will confess it so, and speak no more. But now, I will speak.

for Pope John Paul II

Of course I know that all is in a flux. Standards are dissolved. Names alter. Everything is changing. No Bible, no version, no text can abide without alteration.

Now, we learn, it is no more Roman Catholic; all concede, it is just Catholic. It is no longer the mass, no more holy communion, it is the Eucharist. It is not the Pope we are to see, no more the Holy Father, but the 'first among equals', the 'first bishop of Rome'.

England is, we are told, and told by Rome, 'Mary's dowry' to the papacy. Mary? But in our history books she was Bloody Mary to us, and England — far from Mary's dowry — was Henry's legacy and Elizabeth's heritage. Latimer's flaring torch was not put out, nor Sir Richard Grenville's *Revenge* unavenged.

But above all, we had been taught, Protestants appealed to the Bible, and papists to their traditions.

Now, change of changes, it is the Protestants who must cast off their traditions, and the papacy that appeals to the Bible! This is marvellous in our eyes. In the bewildering kaleidoscope of changes by which we have been at once disorientated only to discover new changes on their way even before the breath be caught: it is all passing strange. We have not heard it on this wise before.

But be it so, Pope John Paul II, after all, you send us to scripture, be it so: then questions arise. An appeal has been made and a great question arises.

Hast thou appealed unto scripture? Then unto scripture thou shalt go.

9

If it be said, No, but that sounds like protesting prejudice; I deny it. Far from Protestant prejudice I had absolutely no church background whatever. After leaving a rich and atheistic home I went into the Merchant Navy, not the church. We were told, the fool went to the army and the dunce to the church. Literally I detested and loathed the 'church' and because of it, all that the church was supposed to represent. Held it in contempt.

Till I was converted I never went near a church. But only then, having been called by grace, then I went. And was staggered at what I saw and found.

Then indeed I sought the Lord alone. Seven years at one stretch I lived a recluse, all day, every day, alone, praying and studying my Bible, crying and calling upon God for light and help. Apart from this seclusion, I went only to the mountains to pray. Since then, again, three years more.

Did then I learn by tradition? Did I belong to a sect? Did I? Then in my loneliness, surely I would have joined those that held it! But truly, I feared to be with men lest I should be led astray by their traditions and compromises. So I was moved in the solitary places, yearning and striving for tenderness of heart before the Spirit of the Lord. O that I might learn of him. That I might hear a voice behind me when I turned to the right hand or to the left — and often I did turn to the right hand and to the left — 'This is the way: walk ye in it.'

No doubt I shall be condemned for independence, conceited singularity or worse — the jargon of psychology becomes the new arsenal of the false witness — but not, Sir, Protestant prejudice. This is not the voice of party prejudice. My conscience bears me witness. And I believe and pray, neither yet is it the voice of singular conceit. Much less that of their psychological claptrap.

Well then, this is my question: Since you have appealed to the Holy Scripture, to which all these years I have been given — with prayer, fasting and solitary vigil — to searching with the uttermost of my measure; and since I find a disparity between what you say and that scripture to which you have sent us, am I wrong, then?

Am I wrong? For I believe that I see much — and much fundamentally — that is incompatible with those scriptures to which I am sent. Then, if I am wrong, I beg your correction. If it be so, please set me to rights.

Now I shall ask — and bear with me if I ask in what we call, plain English — and do you consider.

First of all there is this question of Rome.

This geographical prominence, whence comes it? Rome, you tell us, has supremacy; and moreover the 'first bishop' — the pontiff — sits supreme in that ascendancy over all other churches. It is true that now this pre-eminence is called 'the first among equals'. 'First bishop' out of many. Only it is not subtle qualifications but the thing qualified about which I wish to ask you.

So you are appealing to scripture. But the question is, is this justified by scripture? Not according to my knowledge. Then tell me?

Rome. In scripture, Sir, as to 'Romans', the citizens of Rome, the people, I find eleven references. All in the New Testament of course. First in the gospel according to John, the other ten references from the pen of Luke in the Acts of the Apostles.

But it is not the citizens that concern us, is it? It is the city, Rome itself. And what distinguishes that city. Or what you say distinguishes it. Like 'the first bishop' of Rome. Authority for which now sends us from tradition to scripture.

The city of Rome is referred to nine times. Six times in the Acts. Twice reference to Rome is found in the Epistle to the Romans. Finally there is one mention in the second Epistle to Timothy.

Apart from this there is the Epistle to the Romans itself, an epistle of unparalleled importance, sixteen chapters in all of absolutely vital significance. It is the epistle revealing the saving gospel of Christ. In this it has no equal. Therefore to this book of course presently we must return with our question.

For now, I note the references to Rome. The nine references.

Only nine?

But is there not a rule of proportion in scripture? What of the claims of Jerusalem with over one hundred and forty New Testament references, let alone the hundreds of others mentioned in the Old Testament? Does not the very proportion in which a place is mentioned indicate something of the relative significance in which it was held?

So where is Rome in relation to Jerusalem in the New Testament? Nine to over one hundred and forty!

for Pope John Paul II

And Peter was at Jerusalem. He is never — no, not ever — mentioned as being even near — much less at — Rome. Not in scripture. Not in the New Testament. And the question is, you have sent us to the New Testament, Pope John Paul II.

Then how can you account for the utter insignificance of Rome, spiritually? And the total absence of Peter from that place, in any reference from any verse in any book in the entire New Testament scripture? Tell me?

Anyway, as to the significance of any one earthly location over another — and the numerical significance is without doubt in favour of Jerusalem — as to *spiritual* things, it is utterly despised. The apostle Paul, in the Epistle to the Galatians, finally dismisses Jerusalem 'below', leaving absolutely no room for any New Testament alternative or successor.

Jerusalem's day was over, for all its sacred tradition reaching back into the mists of time. Before Rome was even a dream.

The apostolic writings pour contempt on the very idea in principle of any place in the world being supreme in the church. The Holy Ghost dwells without distinction in all the churches. Christ in heaven takes central place, spiritually, for the whole church and from every one of the churches. Equally, over all the earth.

Jerusalem was the one place that might seem to have had claim, from the Old and in the New Testament. But he speaketh on this wise, dismissing the very idea:

'Jerusalem which now is,
and is in bondage with her children.'

13

A Question

As to a people in Christ, the true church, he has another thing to say as to where they should look for authority. There is a place, yes. But it is utterly in contrast with anywhere on earth:

'Jerusalem which is above
is free, which is the mother of us all.'

Jerusalem above, observe: in heaven. Not Jerusalem below on earth. No, not for all her distinction. For the time was come — with the introduction of the new testament — that no longer at Jerusalem would men worship. Why not? Because in contrast with earthly grandeur and traditional location:

'They that worship the Father
must worship in spirit and in truth.'

These words of Jesus, observe, are in direct contrast with the very idea of geographical supremacy in the Christian religion and church.

And if not Jerusalem, then how much less Rome which cannot put two figures together to make a claim? That is, from scripture. For you have sent us from tradition to scripture, Karol Wojtyla, and that is the question.

Peter at Rome? Then why is there no evidence for it? In scripture? You may say, But we have evidence. I reply, But not from scripture. Not a shred of evidence in the Bible. The New Testament silence is palpable. Not a word, not a hint, not even an allusion to Peter being at Rome.

Yet if it mattered to the early church whether Peter ministered and died at Rome, would not the scripture say *something?* But it says nothing.

14

Then how much more should scripture say something if it not only mattered but were vital, as you say, absolutely vital to the ages of the church thereafter? For Peter to have founded a perpetual authority over all the churches, the entire church, from Rome, it would be imperative to have the most unequivocal direction from Holy Scripture. But there is not one single word.

Yet if this matter were so important to God, to the Father, to the Son of God, to the Holy Ghost, to the apostolic church itself, as you say it is, and as you insist absolutely, then why no word from him? In scripture? For if Roman supremacy be true, must not scripture have declared so? Yet scripture, the New Testament, the apostles, are all totally silent about it.

And in the trifling total of nine references to Rome, at no time is Peter either mentioned or connected with that city. Moreover in none of the references is Rome itself in any way marked out as having the least spiritual significance.

Why then is the New Testament silent about that on which the Roman Catholic church is so vociferous? And that constantly? On which you and your system depend? Why?

Why? Because what has been built up by the traditions of men since scripture closed is nothing whatever to do with the apostles or what they purposed for the church in the future, whilst scripture was open. Least of all did it matter to Peter. Whilst any of the apostles were still alive, that is, while epistles were still being written, to the very last, Rome was as irrelevant in fact as it is now unauthenticated by holy writ.

The scripture — to which you have sent us — finds Rome ignored completely by Peter in his epistles and over the whole written chronicle of his entire life and ministry. Not one single connection. In scripture, that is. Of course, tradition is something else again.

The only valid record of the apostle Peter's life is that testified by the Holy Ghost and is what is recorded by the writers of the New Testament within the confines of Holy Scripture. Peter lived and died within the period of the writing of these New Testament books.

I repeat, there is no mention of his having ministered at Rome and there is not even any record of his having been there. Now were your tradition, so important to Roman Catholicism, as important to the LORD, it must, but must, absolutely must have been in the record of scripture.

That it is not in the scripture shows that what is vital to Roman Catholicism — because your church and ministry is founded upon it — *did not exist* in New Testament times. There appears in scripture another kind of ministry and a totally different kind of church.

That is obvious.

So that I cannot see how you have served your cause, or your evangelical Anglican friends have served your cause — for they long to be with you — by this appeal to scripture. It has nothing but the opposite to the effect you desire, so far as I can see.

Then there is the question of the 'first bishop' of Rome, a precedent you claim to have been established by

Peter. But I have shown it could not possibly have been established by Peter, not at Rome, for he was never there, no, not in all scripture.

However, what is this about 'bishops'?

'Bishop' of Rome? This statement confounds gift and office, according to scripture.

The apostles — and others too — were comparatively rare 'gifts' of ministers given from the ascended Christ, by the Holy Ghost below, to the entire church, but not for any limited or particular location. Though the apostles were to begin at Jerusalem, it was only 'begin'. Thereafter they were to go to the uttermost parts of the earth.

These 'gifts' from Christ on high were quite a different thing — and not to be confused with — the much more numerous gifts of the Spirit within the body, that is, in a church at any given location.

Because scripture never speaks of — and there is no such thing as — the apostle of Jerusalem, the minister of Rome, or the apostle at the church in Corinth. For the simple reason that the sum of the 'gifts' of ministry from on high were sent by the Son of God to the whole church of God for the entire work of God in all the body of Christ.

These gifts from heaven were not given to any one of the churches in particular or to any special area or location. They were sent to and for the whole body of Christ on earth. That was one of the essential differences between the old testament and the new. Between Judaism centred on Jerusalem below, and the church holding fast the Head, that is, the Son of God in glory.

17

A Question

Wherefore he saith,

> 'When he ascended up on high ...
> he gave gifts unto men ...
> and he gave some, apostles;
> and some, prophets;
> and some, evangelists;
> and some, pastors and teachers.'

To do what?

> 'For the perfecting of the saints.'

All of them in general; not a city or a diocese of them in particular.

> 'For the edifying of the body of Christ.'

Not a part of it in a given locality or even some special country, but the whole body in all the world, wherever that body was located.

Hence gifts are ministry sent to the whole church and all the churches without distinction throughout all the world. There is no such thing in scripture as the minister of such and such a church. Or of seminaries in the world 'qualifying' ministers. Here the 'reformed' adaptation of the Roman system is nothing but unreformed tradition. Nor is there anything in scripture of making one church a centre for all the others. Or one central assembly. That is pure Judaism.

The ministers of God are sent from Christ to the church as such and to all the churches equally, and never anything less. Not in scripture.

Neither Protestantism nor nonconformity ever grasped

this truth. Inadvertently, Methodism came near it at the beginning. Quakers were perhaps nearest. As to Brethren, they have scorned the entire conception of the ministry; but Darby never taught this, at first.

So much for gifts sent to the churches. What of 'office'?

As to 'bishops'—a bastardised transliteration in English— these were not the gifts of ministers and ministry to be recognised as sent from Christ to the whole church. Nor were they gifts of the Spirit within the body in a given church. Much less does the word refer to some individual over a diocese or group of churches.

'Bishops' themselves — always plural, never singular — did not choose each other but were chosen by the apostles and their ministers. The Lord having sent his ministers and blessed the ministry of the gospel in a given place, the church was thus raised up in that place. Then the 'bishops' were to be chosen on the basis of their being men well known for their reputation and character in the locality. There was no question of their being gifts, or even having them: it was for their character that men chose them.

This plurality of 'bishops' occurred, then, within any one of the churches and was charged with its singular government. But not the government of any other. No question of their being 'clergy', or of one of them being over a district of churches. Absolutely not. Simply, they were a group of older men within a given church, chosen on the ground of their integrity and maturity.

It is a question of ordinary working men, believers, of impeccable character, elders, older men, being appointed in the plural by such as Peter or Paul, Timothy or Titus, for the work of oversight and government within that local church in particular.

That is the scripture. Abbreviated, it is true. But still the scripture, Pope John Paul II, and what puzzles me is, why ever have you appealed to it to justify a system to which it is utterly a stranger?

I beg the Pope not to dismiss these as light words, or swiftly spoken.

God is witness of what I can only call agonies of soul and spiritual exercise. They are written after decades of wandering up and down as in a dry and thirsty land, years of profound interior distress.

And over what?

Over nothing else than the vision of the true doctrine of Christ, over the true body of Christ, the house of God, the bride of the Lamb, as witnessed in scripture but, alas! lost to view at this present.

For I do not think doctrine by any means so reformed as many suppose. In fact I believe it is utterly beclouded.

Perhaps, at first, most of all my agonising was over the true ministry. Because fidelity to what I saw left me without a ministry which I could conscientiously join or enter. Agonising exercises then, over a ministry in scriptural times evidently sent directly from the LORD in glory, ascended in heaven, a ministry anointed with power from on high, a ministry answering to and resulting in that one body on earth, full of the Holy Ghost indwelling below.

Yet a ministry the like of which eluded the Reformers and Protestants as much as the Roman Catholics.

Agonies, Pope John Paul II, agonies.

For what appears — and appears just as much in Protestantism, in the 'free churches' of so-called nonconformity, in the proud little 'biblical' sects; and what actually disappears in the worst of all, the modern 'Brethren', anarchists who hate the very idea of all authority in the church, and detest even the conception of any Ministers whatsoever — what appears is a mass of titles, honours, medieval affectations of dress, collars, gowns, long robes, covetousness, worldly learning and fleshly pride appropriately clothed yet expressly forbidden by the lips of the Lord Jesus himself.

And in all this, I confess, I by my pride once sinned and took my part both on the one hand and on the other.

O may the LORD pardon what we have all done to what he had left when he ascended on high. The LORD pardon.

What agonies of soul over the one body, the church; oh, only the years can tell.

Rome, or perhaps for us the Church of England, alone presenting at least some tangible answer to oneness, to authority, to apparent unity. Some facsimile of one exterior form of the church and, equally important, one ministry. But how far short of the scripture?

Oh, lonely agonies!

And most because the professing 'believers', the supposed 'evangelicals' seemed not to *care* about these things.

Not to care. To them they were irrelevant. Worse, they were 'divisive'. They upset people. Nothing to do with Christianity as they saw it with their flippant, jolly, over-simplification. Their indifference to Christ and his interests early taught me 'there is no fear of God before their eyes.'

Oh! Agonies.

The contemporary tradition so tangible; the heavenly doctrine so interior. The visible system so accessible; the visionary concept so elusive. The formal unity so plausible; the spiritual union so divine.

Compromise so easy; traditionalism so accepted; the actualities so unquestioned. Faith so rare; idealism so mocked; spirituality so nebulous.

Crucifying. The way so hard; the way so utterly *lonely*. Oh, agonies, Karol Wojtyla, agonies. Temptation past flesh and blood to resist: to trade the church that is for the church that is not, the things that can be seen for the things that cannot, to trade the existent policy for the spiritual perfection is past flesh and blood.

But not past the cross. Not past the Spirit. Not past the power of God.

It was not that one had no opportunities: to me the conventions of the evangelicals were opening. I spoke at perhaps one of the largest: and the prospect was opened without limit in such circles. I preached 'with a view', as they say, at the most coveted of many of the churches. My correspondence will witness to these calls. It was I that forsook them, not the other way round. For even on the very platform — the ideal of the preacher reached — I felt cold as ice within myself. I knew the testimony of God was against this that avoided every real and spiritual issue. The Spirit witnessed with my spirit, and I left everything, not knowing whither I went. Save, as many as are led by the Spirit of God, these are the sons of God. This was to worship the Father in spirit and truth. Even if the vision of the church and ministry was not realised in fact, I was to pray for it, wait for it and abide by it, no matter the cost. And it was a cost.

Evangelicalism, you know, is a fostered and exploited illusion divorced from reality. Evangelicals unite in various activities, conventions, crusades, 'all one in Christ Jesus', for two or three weeks a year, and quite willingly forget the actual divisions to which they really belong. For they are separated members of divided bodies. It is to these that they belong in practice, and by which they are divorced one from another not only for two illusory weeks but in all their real existence.

For evangelicals repudiate any attempt to answer to Christ's vision of one body, one church, by their actually clinging to distinct denominations and sects. By a variety of excuses they shut their eyes from either seeing or seeking for the one body and the one house of God.

Just as they tolerate a system of inventing, manufacturing and hiring ministers on a denominational basis clean contrary to the word of God. Whilst of course loudly professing that word, scorning the very 'Romanism' to which they owe so much of their practice.

Oh, evangelicals are past masters at hiding the truth from themselves by fixing their gaze exclusively upon their agreed criteria bolstered by occasional common activities.

Meanwhile an engineered amalgamation is taking place parallel with this fragile delusion. True to their tradition and type this is blithely ignored by the 'evangelicals'. Nevertheless it is the actuality of the denominational intercommunion of which 'evangelicals' are a very real part, and for which they must bear equal responsibility.

One day their transient dreams will be rudely awakened by this reality of which they have taken no notice. The reconstruction of Christendom will have taken place. Rome will be supreme. Their incorporated denominations will be a part of this communion. And tokens of loyalty will surely be required of her members.

Then what will they say? I know what they will say. They will say, Give us of your oil; for our lamps are gone out.

Agonies, Pope John Paul II. I cannot express how deep was my distress over the one body of Christ, the one unity of the Spirit.

Eventually feeling that the fact of visible unity must — perforce — override everything else, I approached the Church of England, as representing that unity in this country. Meeting with and opening my heart to the then Lord Bishop of Oxford, I found him ready to welcome me into Anglicanism. But also anxious enough to acquire my own spiritual knowledge to support his arguments for Anglican-Methodist reunion.

However, he appeared to me massively indifferent to the thought of biblical repentance on the part of the church, and really contemptuous of the very idea of *true spiritual recovery* from out of the ruins we and our fathers had made. To him — and so heart-broken was I, that, I confess, almost to me — the actual state of the outward denominational position was the reality, and the rest: hopeless dreams of idealism.

However, the effect of his cynicism, of his unbelief in the attainability of the spiritual vision, was to strengthen, not weaken, my own wavering faith.

I saw that this was precisely the temptation to the Jewish Christian, looking back at the outward glory of Israel in the Epistle to the Hebrews. It is a spiritual temptation over the comparison between visible religion endorsed by worldly glory, and the poverty and suffering of invisible, despised and spiritual Christianity.

So that even at that very moment I was strengthened. Anew I determined to suffer affliction with any of the people of God I could find. And if I could find none, then even so not to waver, but to suffer alone. Not to accommodate the profession of Christ to ecclesiastical and denominational conformity to this world, but go out of the world, confessing myself a stranger and a pilgrim upon the earth. And when I find one or another in this way, I know that I have discovered others of the faithful remnant of the church.

And is this unscriptural, or scriptural?

For there is a remnant, isn't there?

Not Protestantism, of course, and not the Free Churches, as they call themselves; nor can such a remnant yet be found as a gathered and united people. Although the various house-meetings and several organised attempts might like to think so. No, not gathered into the unity of one body, nor even yet conceiving the truth of it.

Nevertheless, a poor remnant sighs and groans in the dark.

Yet not the church but the ministry comes first. The ministry must come first. It was not the Acts of the Church, much less the Acts of the Brethren. It was the Acts of the Apostles. An unfinished book. For to this day, the ministry must gather the saints.

Meanwhile 'Protestant' leaders, these priests and clergy and — as men say — ministers, lead their denominations and the heirs of Protestant sects back to the city whence they came out. Just waiting the right moment, a suitable weakness, a fluctuation, to deliver their charges into full intercommunion with Romanism. And the deceitful 'evangelicals' in the midst. All this is true. But it is not scriptural.

Pope John Paul II, it is not scriptural. Nor honest. Not even honest.

If Rome be right, then let these people individually act on conscience and join Rome for their own part.

However, the evangelical leaders claim that their corporate creeping is scriptural. But it is not. 'Let every man be fully persuaded in his own mind.' Let a man act on his own conscience, not beguile others. Yet simple honesty will not do for the ambition of these climbers. No, they must lead their entire sect, all the dreaming evangelicals, all denominations together, into what is referred to as a new concept of the churches' unity, a new renaissance in

which the Word, Authority and the Sacraments appear in a
new light, a light — we are told — fully to justify the elastic
evangelical alliance with 'fellow believers of different
persuasion'.

Now, we all know that 'Word' occurs everywhere in
the Bible. And since their labour consists in showing us
how biblical appears the new Catholicism, therefore our
evangelical denominationalists must present many texts, a
host of scriptures, and frequently refer us to this 'Word'.

However, the corollary of 'Word' is 'preaching'. And
preaching only.

Preaching? Preaching only? Sir, Roman Catholicism is
essentially sacramental. Surely?

So, to tranquillise the fears of the laity, these clergymen
superimpose much irrelevant, inapplicable and immaterial
scripture upon their arguments for union under the 'first
bishop of Rome'. Indeed, going further than Rome ever
intended, they would paperhang the pages of the New
Testament all over the walls of the Vatican till nothing but
scripture appears. Yet to add faith alone in the gospel to
a sacramental system is to build a tottering wall with
untempered mortar indeed. But for the evangelicals to take
to this daubing, well Sir, it must make you smile, after
all.

However, it is easy to perceive that sacramentalism
remains essentially what it ever was, and seemingly always
will be under the rendering and wallpapering.

It is quite true that the outward appearance has altered.
The scriptures and the gospel are plastered and papered

over the edifice, but this is as superficial as it is really impossible. Because such an addition is made to serve no purpose other than to justify a system which in essence — and this is the rule — you will never allow to be touched or altered.

To achieve a change of appearance in what must never be altered requires a certain dexterity. Evidently it is the scripture that must be made to adapt. But at what cost? Necessarily the heart of the gospel must be torn out. The life of it must be sacrificed on the altar of sacramentalism around which its remaining textual fragments are made to drape.

And this is the 'new' appearance? The inspiration for the 'new' unity?

But it will not do: it is all forced. Scripture can never be adapted to a system which in essence professes to convey Christ to the people by sacraments through the works of the clergy. Because the true gospel, the apostolic gospel, the scriptural gospel in very principle is one which conveys Christ by preaching through faith alone. And it is to this that the 'Word' is appropriate; sacrament is not; the very idea of a priesthood over the people quite gone out with the old testament. As to preachers, these must be the gift of Christ from heaven, verified by the testimony of the Holy Ghost on earth, and not otherwise. 'Not of men, neither by man.'

Now, that is scriptural, and brings in the church.

If you say, Where is it? I confess, not in Protestantism; not the Free Churches; neither the proud little sects; nor in the vast majority of the gospel halls. The truth is — and they refuse to admit the truth — we have sinned and our

28

iniquity is very great. It is precisely this real and heartfelt repentance that is so missing from the bright showmanship of modern evangelism.

However, to return to Rome. That is, to the Rome mentioned in scripture, of course.

'Rome' occurs nine times, I observe.

Take the Acts. For example, strangers of Rome were at Jerusalem. Claudius commanded all Jews to depart from Rome. Paul the apostle knew by the Spirit 'I must also see Rome.' Not, Peter knew; Paul was the one who knew. Not Peter, the apostle to the circumcision; naturally not. It was the apostle to the uncircumcision of course, Paul. The LORD says to the one sent expressly to the Gentiles — as opposed to Peter sent to the Jews — 'Paul, *thou* must bear witness at Rome also.' Hence Paul 'went towards Rome', and found brethren. And he 'came to Rome', and preached the gospel under restricted conditions. Well, that was to be expected at Rome. Six references in all to Rome from the Acts of the Apostles.

Once more in Second Timothy referring to an occurrence concerning Paul at Rome.

The other two references are in the Epistle to the Romans. Romans 1:7, 'To all that be in Rome, beloved of God' the apostle Paul writes, preaching and teaching the gospel of Christ in his epistle. Here above all he is 'ready to preach the gospel to you that are at Rome also', Romans 1:15.

And what does he preach? That is the question. What does he advocate as the gospel?

For here is scripture, and scripture for Rome and to the Romans, with a twofold witness. Then surely it is this, and this exactly, and this without any adulteration, that we should hear *from* Rome in the name of all that is apostolic? But do we hear it?

What do we hear and what do we not hear from Rome today?

Please permit me, in your courtesy, permit me to speak with English bluntness all that is in my heart. And if it is forthright, see in this, I beseech you, no impudence, but a genuine anxiety to be clear, open and guileless in speech. In such a spirit, then, I continue to declare what I see, and to pursue my question.

As I perceive it, in order to understand Paul's writing and teaching and hence his laying the apostolic foundation of the Christian church, it is just as important to notice what was not said at Rome. What was not written in the Epistle to the Romans.

What is omitted from the entire sixteen chapters?

Well, bishops, for a start.

Not one single bishop. Never was only one anywhere, of course. Not in scripture. Always in the plural these, elderly men from among the congregation. Working men, they were together in the church concerned in the place where they worshipped with their brethren. That is, where they laboured and lived their lives.

These 'bishops' had been chosen to the oversight over the congregation by the ministers whom Christ had sent

—for example, Paul, Silas, Titus or Timothy — who had
preached the gospel to them, which also they had believed.
Now unlike the oversight of elders, this apostolic ministry
was of course to the whole church, not just to that one
church in which those particular bishops had charge.

For the ministers sent by Christ were to set apart
bishops in every church so as to safeguard for the future
the preaching and teaching of the gospel in its order and
worship. Throughout the whole church the preachers of
the gospel were to set apart bishops in every one of the
churches. The 'bishops' were to oversee the congregation,
the more especially in the absence of the ministers. These
overseers were to have a certain character. Such as being
the husband of one wife, Sir, not none.

Nevertheless, I digress; for none of this is the concern of
the Epistle to the Romans.

Romans is too fundamental for such peripheral things as
bishops and deacons.

It is the gospel over which they are to watch that is the
present — and pre-eminent — concern. Not yet the watchers
or the caring. It is the thing cared for: the gospel itself.
Because of that fact, there are no bishops in Romans. The
word is not mentioned.

So however could this novel idea of one bishop in
particular occur? Especially at Rome, you understand?
Because even the proper appointment of the plural oversight itself does not find a place in the Roman epistle.

Romans is the doctrine that founds and forms the
church. And that of course precedes the order in which it

is governed once founded. Believing that doctrine, the congregation was formed into and was constituted that church by the Holy Ghost. That was the church.

The church never was a kind of depository of salvation to be dispensed by sacraments through a clerical priesthood. Absolutely unknown in scripture. Absolutely contradicted by scripture. Neither did the church itself teach. The church was taught. The church was taught by the ministers; it did not do the teaching.

A very different Rome here, then.

But surely, when in Romans, we ought to do what the Romans did? Not do what they never even read. Well, what they never read at Rome necessarily is conspicuous by its absence from the Epistle to the Romans.

Strangely, in this epistle there is no church.

No 'church at Rome' is mentioned. On the contrary, the letter is addressed, Romans 1:7, to 'all that be in Rome, beloved of God.' That is, the election. Because, you see, that was before the church.

Election comes first. But you are rather wary of that at Rome since Calvin, aren't you? Even the name Calvin makes cardinals jump a bit, and popes narrow their eyes, over there in Rome, doesn't it?

Fear not from me; I do not need to dig up dead men's bones to rattle at you: their day is gone. It is from the living God I got my faith and my ministry, and, man to man, I speak to you as we are: not as they were. I have no time to live in the past: good or bad — it has gone for ever till the judgment day. But election has not.

Then they are — ch. 1:7 — 'called saints'. Called saints, these beloved of God. That is, all the believers at Rome, the elect, the beloved of God, were called saints.

Now, if it were possible for the apostle to send a letter to Rome today to those 'called saints', it would be delivered severally to coloured pictures, carved icons, plaster images, stone statues and wooden effigies. Gilded no doubt, but then, that's an old religious custom; the point is, these 'saints' would be dead images.

But 'the living, the living, he shall praise thee, as I do this day.' And in the Epistle to the Romans, the living believers without exception did all praise him, and were all called saints. In scripture.

Well, how do you account for that, who send us to scripture to justify contemporary Rome?

Now, I observed that the addressees are not called the church in the Epistle to the Romans. Why not? Because they show — who were before 'beloved of God' from eternity, and thereafter 'called saints' to everlasting — they show forth the very first causes. The believers show, by their having received through faith alone that sole doctrine contained in the epistle, what constitutes the church. When they believe that, then they, they, Sir, are the church.

No question of stones or buildings being called 'churches'. How can a building believe?

No question of sprinkled water miraculously ensuring the future belief of irrational babies. As if it did!

No question of steeplehouses, masshouses, priesthouses or cathedrals essential to the very beginning of your system. For God dwelleth not in temples made with hands, and, What house will ye build me? saith the Lord.

Here *the gospel by faith only* was *the whole of the apostolic system.* And they who believed it were the church. Hence, 'To all that be in Rome, called saints.'

And they were saints. No question of believing without regeneration. They believed *from* regeneration. God had made them holy. They were a truly sanctified people, individually, inwardly, outwardly, and as a company. That is why God indwelt them, in Father, Son and Holy Ghost. And God did indwell them. That was what made them the church. They were sanctified. Called saints. Made holy in love. As to the why and how of God's indwelling, it was through the faith of God's elect. As to the object of that faith, it was in Christ, as set forth in the doctrine of Romans.

We ought to consider that saving doctrine in Romans.

Before papist or Protestant or Free Church brethren appeal to scripture — and Romans in particular — they should consider that there are neither choirs, baptisms, marriages, burials, services, altars, fonts, meetings, conventions, campaigns, Sunday schools, nor any of the paraphernalia on which modern Christendom relies. And without which it would be destitute, lost and bewildered: in a word, for the first time well on the way to heart repentance.

In this apostolic epistle to the Romans there are no priests, save all saints. The virgin Mary is not mentioned. Creeds are not. No such thing. It was the gospel that was credited. Nor is there any liturgy. Nor are sacraments mentioned in the epistle.

There are no sacraments in Romans.

The word does not occur, much less what you call sacraments. The supper, eucharist, mass, communion, ordination, anointing, marriage, last rites, christening: not a word of it in Romans.

In Romans, *believing the gospel conveys Christ*, and believing the gospel alone. After that, come the ordinances.

And only after them, came the corruption of the ministry into priesthood, the transubstantiation of ordinances into sacraments, and conjuring of the congregation into bricks and mortar. But all that is *outside* scripture. And you have sent us to scripture.

And, as you can see, to scripture we are going.

All this of course is plain English. Do not mistake it for impoliteness. Foreigners sometimes make mistakes about us, you know. For we English are a plain-spoken people who are of Henry's legacy and Elizabeth's heritage. But not rude, Sir. Only, we will have plain truth. What we call, gospel truth.

I mentioned, Sir, that I had spent many years in solitude, praying and searching the scriptures. First, the books of the New Testament — and a few of the Old — then the doctrine running in rich veins throughout these books and of course rooted in the Old Testament.

Before these years of rigour and discipline I had of course read and studied religious writers fairly widely. In fact I had been in the Congregational ministry. But seeing the glaring disparity between Holy Scripture and the church and ministerial system in which I found myself, I left behind my church, ministry, salary, manse, gown, collar, title and pre-eminence over the congregation, and set my face towards the wilderness to seek the Lord.

I was determined to learn of him, or die in the attempt. I was not to learn from man, nor did I. Albeit since then I have found many to confirm — either from the spiritual nature of their conversion, or from the testimony of experimental older Christians — that the Spirit of God has been my teacher in the scriptures and in the things of God, over first a seven-year and then later a three-year period of exclusive devotion and retreat.

Now regarding the salvation which is in Christ, pre-eminently taught in the Epistle to the Romans, I beg leave to lay before you the conclusions — as exemplified in Romans — to which I have been drawn by so many years of prayer and study in solitude. Are these conclusions scriptural? Tell me. Am I wrong? Then correct me.

I would not have done what I did, and certainly could not have sustained it, had I not been led and kept by the LORD my God. That is my conviction, and it was certainly my providence. I believe I received my teaching from the LORD. I say that knowing by experience how deceitful the heart is, and never more than when self is made the subject. That which I know not, teach thou me.

In my years of searching, I know that I did not seek to please men. There were high degrees and honour to be had, universities of renown, that were not altogether outside my attainment, but from these I turned to seek the honour that comes from God only. I did not labour then, nor do I now, that I might achieve a reputation — God is witness — nor for any other cause than an unutterable yearning to know the truth and to be set free by it; to know it from God; and to know that my conclusions have the testimony of pleasing him alone.

I speak the truth, Sir; from the bottom of my heart I know that I am being entirely honest with you, and my own conscience bears me witness.

And for this cause I beg your attention to the question: tell me if you endorse the conclusions which I reached from the gospel — the very foundation of the doctrine.

There is no question of prejudice or sectarianism. To the contrary. In the years behind this work — of which I propose only the simplest summary of the teaching of Romans — I opened no commentary, considered no other writer, neither did I speak with nor listen to any other man. No, not till, after the years had passed, I was certain that I had been established by God and the Father alone in the truth of the gospel concerning his Son.

Now, I ask you, is this from heaven, or of man? If of man, convince me of error from the same epistle, by a more correct conclusion. But if it be of God, I beg you to own it, to confess and to lead us aright in the word of truth, the gospel of our salvation: for we are speaking of the inevitability of either the immortal bliss or the perpetual misery of our undying souls.

Now, you have constantly used the word 'gospel' and as frequently referred us to scripture. Apparently for your authority. Then why the disparity between your addresses and that gospel? And why the difference between the tenor of what you say and that of the original New Testament scripture?

I have read and reread your addresses at Drogheda, 29th September, 1979; at Phoenix Park and Dublin on the same day. At Galway, Knock and Dublin again on the 30th September, 1979; Maynooth on the 1st October, and Limerick, also. Likewise what you said at Boston Common in the U.S.A.; and in the Yankee Stadium, New York, on the 2nd October, 1979. Battery Park, too, and Philadelphia on the 3rd and 4th, with Chicago on the 5th. Then, also, your speeches at Washington D.C. on the 7th October, 1979. I have read and searched, read and searched. Above all, I read and searched your address to the United Nations, New York, 2nd October.

Yes Sir, fair words; humanitarian words; words that touch the chords of humanity, that resonate in matters of this present life, of the sanctity of life, of social responsibility, of moral obligation, of earthly justice. But all concerning the affairs of this present time, the world that now is: I own it, you speak fair, I gladly admit that.

But what of the Lord's return, the end of the world, the next life?

What of sin, guilt, the fall, the state of man in Adam?

What of the certainty of the immortality of the soul?

Of the resurrection from the dead?

What of the dread day of judgment, the last judgment?

But what of the wrath to come?

for Pope John Paul II

What of the curse of the law of God, of everlasting torment?

What of the bottomless pit, the undying worm, the fire unquenchable?

What of the agonising question above all questions:

How shall man be just with God?

Of these things, and God's answer to these things, the gospel treats in general and the Epistle to the Romans in particular.

But so far as I can see — you who came from Rome and should exemplify Romans — you ignored them.

You ignored these weightier matters of the world to come to tithe the mint, anise and cummin of the world that now is.

Or if not quite ignored them: taking them for granted as dismissed by the outward forms and rites — unjustified by scripture — of what you call the 'sacraments' — unknown to scripture — of infant baptism, confirmation and the mass. None of which can or will deliver from the wrath to come. No, not according to the gospel or the scripture to which we have been referred for authority.

Yet not to proceed to the deliverance, simply to be honest about the slavery and bondage of men. Why not a word of the fall, the transgression, sin, wrath, the resurrection, the judgment to come?

What! Has the rationalism, humanism, modernism, liberalism and universalism that has corrupted the high places of all the denominations tempered Rome also?

39

A Question

Would the world be too disgusted at such primitive speech?

Then it would be too disgusted at the gospel, because it would repudiate the sole and only reason for that gospel: the guilt of all the world and our universal condemnation before God in the day of judgment.

But of this the modern culture, modern education, is utterly contemptuous. And I believe you made sure there was nothing to offend them. So what of this scripture:

'They are of the world:
therefore speak they of the world,
and the world heareth them.

We are of God:
he that knoweth God heareth us;
he that is not of God heareth not us.

Hereby know we the spirit of truth,
and the spirit of error.' ?

I read that we are to 'marvel not if the world hate you.'

But how can it hate what flatters it with general moralising? As if, should the world reach up to that moral standard, it had nothing to fear?

Sir, the world, the whole world, is in dreadful, utter, mortal and immortal danger no matter that it should reach any standard whatsoever. For what things soever the law saith, it saith to them who are under the law: that every mouth may be stopped, and all the world may become guilty before God.

Now when did you tell them that?

Moreover we know that 'the whole world lieth in wickedness.'

But you never said so.

It may be replied, The Pope preached a message of love. It was love and peace, brother; because love draws men, not wrath.

Oh? But draws from what? It is from what, as well as to whom, that the gospel carefully expounds. Whatever we may choose to omit. And omit for reasons of worldly expediency which absolutely negate the very essence of love.

You may reiterate, It is love, not wrath, that draws men to Christ.

And well I know it, Sir. But draws from what? That is what the gospel carefully teaches, which you omitted, and, with respect, I ask why? Besides, that it is love which draws sinners, none knew better than that apostle who called himself the chief of sinners. Nevertheless, directing us as to how that drawing takes place, he says,

'Knowing therefore the terror of the Lord, we persuade men.'

And afterwards — afterwards, Sir — balances this with

'The love of Christ constraineth us.'

So that in his apostolic doctrine he shows first that from which love draws sinners, and next, he to whom they are drawn.

In contrast, however, with this truth, what is increasingly

evident in the entire corrupt ministry and all the fallen churches of our times is that they no longer preach the very reason for there being a gospel at all! They omit the fall, sin, guilt, wrath, the second coming of Christ, the resurrection of the dead, the day of wrath.

And why? Because of worldly expediency, the fear of man, the love of applause, and above all the dread of being ridiculed by a world educated out of all dread of the day of judgment.

However, we have an infallible testimony to the way in which the apostle himself had spoken in the world and drawn sinners to Christ.

This is of course in the Epistle to the Romans. Indeed it is the express purpose of that epistle. Here is a book in which the apostle shows his manner of speaking to a people whom he had never met, in a place to which he had never been, yet in fact hoped shortly to visit. As nearly as possible a parallel in circumstance — if I may say so without impertinence — to your prepared addresses in your recent visits.

Surely here is the apostolic precedent. Here is what to say — what must be said — from the everlasting and unchangeable gospel to the unaltered and immortal souls of men in any and all future conditions, till the end of time.

Surely here, if ever, Romans speaks to Rome, and the apostle to the pontiff? By example and commandment?

But as to how divergent were all your messages — without exception — from this infallible doctrine of the apostle Paul in the Epistle to the Romans, let the world judge!

What a contrast between you!

After his brief introduction and explanatory remarks, the apostle Paul commences his exposition of the gospel of Christ proper, in the eighteenth verse of the first chapter. He cries aloud and spares not: he lifts up the voice like a trumpet. He calls,

> Earth, earth, earth,
> hear the word of the Lord!

This is the gospel, this the evangel, this is the word of the Lord. This is the word of truth, the gospel of our salvation. This is that faith without which none shall be saved. This alone is to be preached in all the world till the end of the world.

That minister is pronounced accursed who fails to preach this doctrine.

> 'If there come any unto you, and bring not this doctrine,
> receive him not.'

Receive not such an apostate, though it were one of the twelve apostles themselves:

> 'Though we'

— cries the apostle Paul from his apostolic heights —

> 'Though we, or an angel from heaven,
> preach any other gospel unto you
> than that which we have preached unto you,
> let him be accursed.'

A Question

Anathema Maran-atha. And, lest any should think these words exclusive to that time, he projects the truth of their solemn warning through time by these epistles unto this present, unto you, Pope John Paul II also, saying,

> 'As we said before, so say I now again,
> If any man preach any other gospel unto you
> than that ye have received,'

— received from the Lord Jesus and the holy apostolate, received from the record of the apostolic doctrine in the holy scripture, received in particular — since it deals with the exposition of that very gospel — in particular from the Epistle to the Romans —

> 'So say I now again,
> If any man preach any other gospel unto you
> than that ye have received,
> let him be accursed.'

But by what words shall we recognise that gospel in its very commencement? When first God opened Paul's lips, how did his mouth show forth his praise?

First the love of Christ? No, Sir. First the judgment of God.

First the Father of mercies? No, Sir. First the Judge of all the earth.

First the cross of Calvary? No, Sir. First the dreadful day of wrath. First these words:

> 'For the wrath of God
> is revealed from heaven.'

> *Romans 1:18.*

44

for Pope John Paul II

The apostolic doctrine, commencing at chapter one verse eighteen, continues until the end of chapter five. After that there are questions, prefaced by the rhetorical 'What then?' The 'then' referring the reader back to the doctrine which had been expounded in the preceding four and a half chapters. Therefore the apostolic gospel is opened as to its very essence in the four and one half chapters beginning half-way through chapter one and concluding at the end of chapter five.

It is a revelation. In fact it is a twofold revelation.

Two things are revealed which before stood in total obscurity. Now both are unveiled. Hitherto darkness covered the earth, and gross darkness the people. But with the revelation of the gospel of Christ, this obscuring veil is rent asunder and the beams of glory illuminate what otherwise could never be seen. No, not world without end.

Nor will such things be seen again, not by our generation, not unless this selfsame revelation of the gospel is preached once more with the Holy Ghost sent down from heaven.

And my question to you, Sir, bringing you — who profess to send us to scripture — to the Epistle to the Romans, comparing all your speeches in every one of your visits, my question to you, Sir, is this: Where is the remotest resemblance? Tell me. Where? Let equity itself judge.

The doctrine of the gospel, the faith once delivered, the apostolic word of salvation established in perpetuity, that which is expounded between Romans ch. 1:18 and ch. 5:21: that doctrine is a twofold revelation.

The world can never know this revelation, unless the

45

ministry raised up of God and sent down from Christ
preach it by the Holy Ghost. Because the world has been
blinded by Satan, lies under darkness, and the veil is upon
their hearts. Then how shall they hear without a preacher?
Or how shall one preach except he be sent?

This doctrine, I say, is a twofold revelation. It is the
same light; however, first one thing is revealed by that light
and then another. And only then. It is to be preached
according to the order in which it is revealed.

This doctrine, falling into two parts, reveals first of all
the need and hence the reason for the gospel. Unless this
first be known, and known by revelation, known within,
known experimentally, what follows becomes vapid and
empty to the hearer. Mere theory.

Because what follows thereafter is the revelation of how
God by Jesus Christ superabounds to meet that need. How
he triumphed in answering entirely, absolutely and for
eternity, all the dreadful case of mankind set forth in the
first part of the doctrine.

And how can that follow, if the reason for its existence
is made to appear non-existent by the silence of the
preacher?

Unless the gospel be preached as it is revealed, in that
order, it is neither gospel, nor preaching, nor is it orderly.
Hence, not apostolic. Precedent, Sir, has been established
by divine, infallible and abiding commandment in the
doctrine of the Epistle to the Romans.

The doctrine falls into two parts.

The first consists of sixty-four verses or something like two average chapters, and in this the apostle declares the revelation of the wrath of God.

'For the wrath of God is revealed from heaven.'

That is the revelation and Paul does not cease from revealing it nor from exploring what is exposed to its searching light, no, not until he reaches the twentieth verse of the third chapter.

The very existence, the emphatic nature and the length of this exposure show that there is a divine order and method to the gospel, and only by its observation can the ground properly — or possibly — be prepared in the hearts of men. The apostle spares no pains; he leaves no stone unturned; he occupies the entire space between ch. 1:18 and ch. 3:20, a lengthy period indeed.

Nevertheless that is the declaration, and the subject must be sustained till all the truth comes to light. Man must thoroughly understand the revelation of the wrath of God, because without that divine light humanity remains in the darkness of this present world, blinded to all that is eternal by the outward show of everything that now appears to sight.

Precisely because man is blind to salvation the first work of revelation in the gospel must be to open his eyes to danger. Man must be enlightened as to his need of salvation. Because 'the wrath of God is revealed.' Without this first, there can be no gospel. Only hypocrisy.

If the bare word, letter or descriptions of the love and sufferings of Christ in the gospel are given without the prior work of the first part of the gospel, men will then profess Christ who are an utter disgrace to him. Men will hold the description of Jesus and his cross whose filthy lives and unclean conversation utterly deny both. Men will belong to the church who know no more of the Saviour than the brute beasts. Men's own hearts will give the lie to their own lips. Men will leave their outward Christ on Sunday morning and, before they cross the threshold that afternoon, will have denied in their hearts all that they professed with their lips. They will be wholly returned to the world in anger and despair, and all week remain destitute of Sunday's transient Christ. Their own consciences bear witness to the truth of this their continual experience.

Only when the disease has been made known, then can the cure be applied. Only after the malady has been determined, then shall appear the remedy. Not before it! Diagnostic and exploratory surgery must precede; this must open up the inner man. Then under the all-searching brilliance of a light from which nothing can escape, no shadow remain, in which the hidden parts lie all exposed to view, then, and only then, but then can the remedy be proclaimed.

So it is with the gospel.

First the revelation of the fearful condition of man upon which

'the wrath of God is revealed.'

Immediately following this, however, appears the revelation of the stupendous salvation of God, the antidote to every woe and the deliverance from all the ills of mankind.

'But now the righteousness of God is manifested.'

48

This also is by revelation alone. Here is the consequent, the great revelation in the doctrine. The light which illuminated the true condition of man is now traced to the source of its beams: It is the Lord! He is the light, and in his light we see light. This is the light of the glory. Five scars he bears in glory. Here is the revelation of the righteousness of God in the gospel. 'For therein' — in the gospel — 'is the righteousness of God revealed.'

It was to this that the prior exposure of the sin of man and wrath of God had been leading: that God might have mercy upon all. 'But now the righteousness of God without the law is manifested,' 3:21. And the unfolding of this manifestation will occupy the apostle until the end of the fifth chapter.

But be it so, did we hear anything even remotely like the first part of this doctrine? Let alone the revelation in the second? In your speeches, Sir? Did we?

Not to look for an exact transcript, nor to limit speech as if it must be drawn from this epistle only. Of course not. But the doctrine is salvation, and it is utterly basic; it is that men may be saved, and the only way they may be saved. Now, all confess this salvation to be the essence of the doctrine in Romans. Though, no doubt, echoed in every other epistle. So, in principle, did we hear its doctrine? Did we, Sir?

God forbid you should think this mere faultfinding or laboured censoriousness. I know that the scorner is consumed, and all that watch for iniquity shall be cut off: that make a man an offender for a word.

But not for a word do we look, but for the heart of

the gospel we search, Pope John Paul II, the heart of the gospel.

Even so, might we not have expected at least once, in however remote a speech, even an aside, to hear these actual words of the apostle: 'the wrath of God is revealed'? Or: 'that every mouth may be stopped, and all the world may become guilty before God. For all have sinned, and come short of the glory of God'? And: 'the righteousness of God without the law is manifested'? Or: 'by faith in his blood'? Or else: 'he was delivered for our offences, and was raised again for our justification'? Even: 'being justified by faith, we have peace with God'?

Why, not a word.

Or did we hear the apostle's pleading tones by your voice, see his tears in your eyes, perceive you labouring to shut up men to the sole mercy of God, by convincing them mightily, and that publicly, of sin, righteousness and judgment?

No such voice of wisdom cried in our streets. Truth was fallen in the street. None wept. The tones were mute. On this, there was silence everywhere. A few jokes, perhaps, for the young people, it may be, that they may see, here is a human jolly fellow after all.

But it is divinity we look for; the word of God; the solemnity of eternity.

Did we hear you reason of righteousness, temperance and judgment to come? Did you cry aloud and spare not, lift up the voice like a trumpet, stand between God and men, the dead and the living, heaven and earth, to stay the plague, God commanding by your voice that all should repent 'because he hath appointed a day, in the which he will judge the world in righteousness by that man whom he hath ordained; whereof he hath given assurance unto all men, in that he hath raised him from the dead'?

And did men tremble? Did that day loom nearer, when they should fly from the wrath of the Lamb, that dreadful day? The day in which the sky shall roll up as a scroll and the elements dissolve in fervent heat. The day in which the earth shall drip away in fire, the hills melt, whilst they cry to the mountains, Fall on us, hide us from the wrath of the Lamb, and from the face of him that sitteth upon the throne.

Did they tremble?

How could they? You never said a word. Not a word. Of course, you made rapport. A little laughter. And applause, naturally. But we are talking about immortal souls and the certainty of everlasting fire: without a hope of safety but in Christ.

No, Sir. None trembled. There was no cause. But there is cause in Romans 1:18 to 3:20; with a vengeance there is cause to tremble. But you did not preach it; you did not cry for them to flee from the wrath to come.

Well, Pope John Paul II, you know that there is fire unquenchable, a bottomless pit; you know there is an undying worm, a resurrection body and an immortal soul; you know that without Christ they perish; you know the revelation of the wrath of God must come first in the gospel; you have the keys of knowledge.

But you did not use the keys. You left the door shut. Ignored. The keys unused. Untouched.

And what I ask, Pope John Paul II, in the name of the God of all grace and the Father of mercies, in the name of Jesus Christ the Lord, in the name of a Saviour God, *why?*

Why? You know.

But I go on with my questioning, laying the ground of what I understand to be the revelation of Christ, and inquiring, Is this what you preached? Or, if I am wrong in your eyes, do not kill me, as your predecessors were so wont to do to such as I — but rather show me. If you do so from scripture, I shall follow meekly enough.

But to proceed.

There follows from chapter three and verse twenty-one right to the end of chapter five, that most wonderful revelation of the righteousness of God. Oh, how marvellous is this manifestation!

> 'But now the righteousness of God
> without the law
> is manifested.'

And so it is.

When the apostle concludes this revelation, he follows it with questions and objections of every sort and from all quarters. But so abundant and fruitful is the yield of this most precious doctrine, that he takes the hypothetical questioner for his reply straight back to this doctrine for an end to all controversy. So that at the last this silences every argument, supplies every answer, puts to flight all objections, shames every disputer and levels all queries to an adoring subjection. It is like the Queen of Sheba before Solomon, trying him with hard questions. There was no breath left in her, and she confessed, The half hath not been told.

Marvellous, oh, stupendous, wonderful gospel. Blessed be God and the Father for grace abounding, glory outshining, divinity surpassing all that tongue can tell, eye may behold, or hath entered into the heart of man to conceive.

Now then, the apostle manifests the mercies of God to men, and on every hand we see the love of God superabounding to meet the helpless guilt of the ungodly. Poor sinners are translated for nothing but faith into a large place, onto new ground altogether, with a totally transformed standing before God in grace: they are seen as justified and as having righteousness and life in Christ. They have done nothing at all. God has done everything in Christ. What has been wrought in them by the interior Spirit of God is faith to believe it. To believe that the grace of God meets man in all his corruption, guilt and danger, as he stands cursed by the law of God, already under condemnation and wrath. Grace abounds to lift the penitent absolutely out of his position and place him entirely in a new standing, sprung out of nothing but the sheer goodness and mere mercy of God.

How personal is this grace!

Romans is an individual matter. It shows what one's own baptism signified: not of course that ridiculous sprinkling of helpless, uncomprehending infants, but that voluntary, intelligent baptism which follows after faith in order to signify what has been believed. 'He that believeth' — first — 'and is baptised' — second — 'shall be saved.' And saith the Lord Jesus to the eleven, 'Go and teach all nations, baptising them.' What, go to their nurseries? Teach in the nurseries, preach to cradles, is it? For whomsoever they are who receive this teaching, these alone are the ones afterwards to be baptised in consequence. Then, since the tradition that has overtaken and sunk the church 'baptises' babies, it would have to follow, these infants were they to whom the Lord sent the apostles to teach.

Unless, of course, your tradition is all wrong. One or the other.

Hence we see that Romans declares that evangelical teaching, of which baptism is the subsequent figure or sign in those that believe and submit. Not that Romans is concerned with the sign. It is not. The thing signified is what occupies our apostle.

What then does baptism signify? It is a figure in which one has been marked out as buried with Christ.

Burial with Christ answers everything that was raised against one in judgment in Romans. The wrath of God was raised against one with perfect justice: now with as equal a justice, God has freely provided, and provided for nothing but faith, the perfect answer.

Believest thou this, Karol Wojtyla? I know that thou believest.

The real issue is, doth God give his free provision by sacraments, through priesthood, and from the church?

for Pope John Paul II

I answer, Nay, BUT BY FAITH ONLY!

And I answer from the apostles from whom — I am careless to say it — you have departed. Why send us to their scriptures then?

This finds out your departure at the heart of it. Come at the heart of it: *in Romans there are no sacraments, there is no priesthood, nor is there any church.* There is only the gospel, and solely faith in that gospel.

I know that you concede the death of Christ and the doctrine of it, but what I discern is where the issue lies exactly: HOW IS THAT DEATH CONVEYED?

Father, Son and Holy Ghost, all heaven, the elect angels, the twelve apostles, the word of God, the scripture of truth, Peter and Paul, all the early saints, the first churches, Zion, the city of the living God, the heavenly Jerusalem, an innumerable company of angels, the general assembly and church of the firstborn which are written in heaven, God the Judge of all, the spirits of just men made perfect, all, all agree in one to submit to the doctrine of Christ given by the holy apostle in the Epistle to the Romans, and so to give the lie to your ecclesiastical false traditions: *it is by faith only.*

Without works. Without sacramental works, priestly works, penitential works, works of supererogation, ecclesiastical works, clerical works, any works; no works at all, but *by faith alone.*

This is what you have defied, and all your followers, isn't it?

A Question

And, to where you crouch unmoved and unmoving, fallen Protestantism is drifting back.

Nor yet has there been a prophetic voice, the voice of the Spirit, a voice from heaven raised up in protest, no, not in our day.

They reprint books to make dead men say what they dare not, today. Cowards! Don't you think so too, Karol Wojtyla? I believe you do, for as a man, and as to manly qualities and character, I admire you very greatly. But we are talking of salvation.

Not a voice in protest. No, not from heaven.

Not yet. But I know that I write this by the Spirit of my God. And I know the consequences to which I expose myself. But I do not fear you, Pope John Paul II. I fear God.

Buried with Christ! Thus good tidings are preached to the meek, the broken-hearted find that which binds them up, liberty is proclaimed to the captives and the opening of the prison to them that are bound. Here is comfort for the mourner, with the ground of consolation founded in vengeance having been requited, justice satisfied, the law honoured and the righteousness of God glorified.

Buried with Christ! This is what is appointed unto them that mourn in Zion, to give unto them beauty for ashes, the oil of joy for mourning, the garment of praise for the spirit of heaviness: that they might be called trees of righteousness, the planting of the Lord, that he might be glorified.

Buried with Christ! More even than being crucified with Christ, here is the fullest answer, the answer to perfection, given freely by God to the sinner to meet his misery and abysmal need. Here I see my identity with Christ in his death. There is nothing against me which that death did not answer, did not silence, and from which it did not obtain absolute and entire acquittal.

Burial includes all this and goes beyond. To this degree: when crucified with Christ, the law, wrath, vengeance, justice itself see to view in the hanging corpse the full satisfaction of every demand. It is seen on the cross. But once buried, nothing remains to view at all. Not a thing can be found. All is gone.

And that is the believer's position in Christ in Romans.

It is true that one sees oneself risen with him in newness of life. Also that the nature of this life is that it is free from the law of sin and death, that it is not under the law but under grace, and that one is alive unto God and filled with newness of Spirit. It is further true that as a result of divine mercies one finds oneself in a company, in one body, with many members.

But these are glimpses; they are consequences. They show the glory beginning to break, the glorious prospect before those who are brought by faith into that place where they are crucified with Christ. And more, the place where his death has been made good to them to the extent that they are seen as having been buried with him and taken out of view. Thus all that could be against them, however militant, of necessity is forced to retire. For there is a total absence of even so much as the fallen corpse of the slain.

This is Roman's answer, and therefore, of course, it is the central Christian position from which all the glory begins to flow.

This is what brings in the body of Christ. It is why the body is glimpsed in chapter twelve. We view the body of Christ as risen with him. Nevertheless Romans, dealing with the individual, is in fact the true evangelist's message. But that message brings, and must bring, the faithful from out of conformity to this world — and its religion — into union with the body of Christ in spiritual harmony.

So that forgiveness of sins, deliverance, justification, propitiation, redemption, reconciliation or ransom cannot be preached nor can they be received in isolation from that to which these things must lead in the nature of the gospel: to one body in Christ. There cannot be continued individualism or independence, because the gospel unites us into one holy congregation with the brethren.

Salvation is preached with an end in view. Our being gathered into the spiritual house of God as a result of believing is in view. Our being gathered out of this present evil world, separated, and gathered together is in view. The church is in view, that which is for the Father and the Son, being indwelt by the Holy Spirit of God.

And this appears at the very last, Romans 16:25, though it is not explained. Nevertheless we are brought so far as to the mystery of the house of God, the congregation indwelt by the Father through the Son of his love, by one Spirit.

This is what the heaven-sent preaching of the true evangel must achieve and will achieve. And maintain.

for Pope John Paul II

It is not maintained by the Lord's supper.

The Lord's supper is not mentioned in Romans; which it certainly would be if some brethren had written it. In fact the only epistle in which the last supper is mentioned is the first of the two Corinthian epistles. Besides this singular silence, one ought to consider the corrective nature of First Corinthians. Had the apostle not been obliged to correct the common meal of that particular congregation, it is doubtful whether any reference to the last supper would have occurred anywhere in the entire apostolic epistles.

Which supper you have — without authority — renamed the mass, or the eucharist. That on which the Roman church, as well as the sacramental Church of England, build their entire system. And now Presbyterians, and I know not who else, are almost indecent in their haste to be incorporated into the first principles of this system.

But what a system is this, that can find but one — corrective — ecclesiastical scripture to justify its existence?

Mind you, these things being so, why are the Plymouth Brethren and their multitude of offshoots and imitators so complacent? For they likewise revolve a system around what they also — without authority — rename 'breaking of bread on Lord's day morning'. Then what reason exists for their separate existence? Certainly neither the inward life nor mighty power of God!

Apart from all this, the Corinthian epistle takes another ground and outlook, altogether different from that of the Epistle to the Romans, or, indeed, of any other epistle.

In Romans, the death of Christ and our death are

59

studied. The epistle opens by finding us alive, guilty, under law and the curse; or without law and condemned by the light of nature as well as that of our own conscience. The whole race is brought in guilty before God, under condemnation and a certain fearful looking for of judgment. But in grace we are found judicially slain in Christ. His blood is seen as satisfying all that the righteousness of God could require or demand. The believer sees entire responsibility met and answered by the Saviour who took it all upon himself and fully discharged everything in our behalf out of nothing but his love towards us as his own people.

How dire was our need! By our own will we stood guilty and condemned before the great Assize. How great is his love! By his own will we stand acquitted and justified before the throne of his grace. And it is through the death of Jesus alone that this translation has been achieved.

God's answer to man's need is death.

Romans is a book about death. But it is the death of Christ. And it is individual and personal: the death of Christ for me, for my sins, for my judgment. As I tremble, alive and responsible, in my guiltworthiness, need and danger, I am met in grace by God who calls me by Jesus Christ to the gospel. A gospel which affords me entire and perfect satisfaction to my very conscience; and what is more and better, it achieves the same entire and perfect satisfaction for God. Then surely God and man can meet here, that is, meet at the place of atonement.

How the truth of the death of Christ is studied in Romans.

His burial is deeply pondered. The Spirit of God broods

over the deep in the shadows of the tomb, and light blazes forth at the command of the word of the Lord. Romans gives the illumination.

What then does one see in the tomb, otherwise so dark, sealed and obscure?

If without conviction of sin, void of the sense of the wrath of God, if never brought to mourn and tremble, if never brought like Mary to the sepulchre: one sees nothing at all.

But if one is spiritually lame, blind, leprous, deaf, dumb, filthy, possessed, as dead, yet quaking for fear of the just recompense for sins: then one sees everything.

One sees cast into the tomb the body of sin, all the filth and corruption of the first man Adam, the sins of the flesh, the fall, death itself, the law, the curse, the day of judgment, hell itself: oh, what relief! Unspeakable. Divine.

Romans is what Paul saw as he stood, as it were, by the grave, in spirit looking into the tomb at the dead body of Jesus. He contemplated. He perceived. He understood. He cried, Our old man is crucified with him! Buried with Christ.

> O death!
> Where is thy sting?
> O grave!
> Where is thy victory?
> Death is swallowed up in victory.

Now who else had seen that so clearly?

But what did Paul see? He saw the flesh, the fall, the world. He saw sin, death, the resurrection of the unjust, the great white throne, the lake of fire: but he saw them all gone, for him. All taken away, disappeared, removed, dismissed and discharged in and through that still and shrouded figure in the sepulchre.

What a death!

Sir, with respect I beg leave to inquire — without the least vestige of impudence — have you stood there personally? For Romans is personal.

If you say, the body is not there now; I answer, *it is there in Romans*. Spiritually. To contemplate. It was there when the two angels sat one at the head and one at the feet, where the body of Jesus had lain. Not there now, no, not physically. It is 'had lain'. But the spiritual truth entailed in his having lain there dead three days, that was what was being contemplated. And may yet be contemplated. It was being absorbed by the angels. All heaven's attention was there. And so was Paul's. And likewise they who read the Epistle to the Romans, crying and praying, hungering and thirsting after righteousness.

But, one may say, the body did not remain in the tomb. No, but like the angels, we should tarry and contemplate, till all is absorbed each for himself. For us, that is to meditate spiritually, to contemplate with profound devotion, to exercise the spirit in prayer without ceasing, in the Epistle to the Romans.

This is the place in the view of heaven where the testimony to the death of Jesus is set forth: 'whom God hath set forth a propitiation' — mercy seat — 'through faith in his blood.' Romans 3:25. There it is to be seen, there at the mercy seat all of gold, cast in one piece with the cherubim, one at the head, the other at the feet of that upon which the blood of atonement was destined to be sprinkled. The figures of the cherubim gaze inward at that sprinkled blood, thereby contemplating, as it were, all the truth that accrued in the dead body in the tomb.

There in Romans, in the mercy seat with the cherubim facing inwards and downwards, there is the spiritual answer to the angels in the tomb, gazing one at the head, the other at the feet, where the body of Jesus had lain.

The apostle in this epistle pauses, gazes inward; he meditates; and meditating, really gains the good of what is ours in the death and burial of Christ.

And, gaining it, writing it, the apostle makes it over to the faith of the believer. That is, the believer of the revelation in Romans. For righteousness of God is revealed in Romans; not to condemn but to justify. Not to be laboured after but freely imputed for faith. Like pure gold, beaten work, it is there. The mercy seat, the propitiatory, the object of spiritual contemplation. The cherubim, all of gold, all one with the mercy seat, enraptured, overwhelmed, eyes for ever gazing at the place where the blood was sprinkled. As it were, one at the head, one at the feet, where the body of Jesus had lain: for the testimony of his death, shed blood, now sprinkled, is there. There it is!

So the apostle gazes within the veil, and so he comes forth from the Holiest of All, from the inmost presence of God, to write the Epistle to the Romans. Revelation indeed: therein is the righteousness of God revealed.

In Romans the faithful are seen with all responsibility met, judicially slain in Christ, and with righteousness of

God freely imputed. All that men lost by the fall of Adam has been recovered and more than recovered by the redemption in Christ. The fall into sin and death is more than answered by the elevation into righteousness and life.

What was set forth in the figure of trees in the garden of Eden really appears in the Epistle to the Romans: access by righteousness obtained to the tree of life, and all obligations answered in respect of the tree of the knowledge of good and evil.

Man clave to that which was forbidden, by works and nature in Adam. And, true to the threat, by sin died in consequence, with disastrous repercussions for the race which Adam represented and whose free will he personified. All was lost on earth, man sold under sin, perdition opened by condemnation and death.

But Christ being come from heaven, appears a tree of life, and a way of access to it besides. The flaming sword of justice having been buried in his side, he opens the way today into paradise, the paradise of God, for every one that believeth.

A far better prospect opens than ever had been lost. A people in Christ are justified by faith, righteousness of a durable everlasting character achieved by the faith of Jesus Christ having been put to their account. It is imputed. It is imputed for faith in his blood. Here is a righteousness, everlasting righteousness, righteousness of God, a righteousness which cannot be lost unless an end can be found to everlasting and a period to the divine being.

The elect — true, real believers — are safe. Christ answers for them. Having obtained their righteousness by his blood, eternal life becomes theirs of course by his gift. Eternal life is freely given. And cannot be lost, unless a boundary can be found to eternity and a mortal pause to the immortality that cannot die.

Since both righteousness and life — more than answering all that was lost in Adam by man — come from God, come by grace and are by faith, then it must follow, faith also is God's gift and God's work. The faith that comes from this interior work of God, the faith of God's elect, can no more perish than the everlasting righteousness and eternal life which call it forth and engage its attention.

Better than Eden in this world, better by far, a new heaven and a new earth in the world to come appear as the element of the faithful. This is their enduring inheritance for ever and ever, world without end, Amen.

Heaven and earth shall pass away, but these words shall not pass away. This is the gospel in the Epistle of Paul the apostle to the called of Jesus Christ, to all that be in Rome, beloved of God, called saints. Grace — saith he to all who obey it and him by faith — grace to you, and peace, from God our Father and the Lord Jesus Christ. Amen.

The saints have righteousness of God imputed freely by grace, where once sin was reckoned of necessity by works. The Spirit is freely given and life imparted through righteousness by Jesus Christ; this supplants the spirit of disobedience within the children of wrath, and death imparted through the transgression of Adam.

The saints are hardly viewed as risen with Christ save at a glimpse, but Christ is seen as risen on their behalf: everything is focused, however, on what is theirs through a serious consideration by faith of the death and burial of Christ. It is all a question of their identity with him and in that. This is what occupies Romans. Where that death has brought them. Whatever else is seen, that is the focus.

Christ is risen for them; they have newness of life, and in it they have seen all that was past put away on the other side of the cross, now taken out of sight in the grave. That is the fresh sight that comes out of newness of life. How clean and clear it is of all that came by nature.

So that although they have the Spirit and are risen with Christ, the spiritual contemplation in Romans is clearly that from which they have risen in him.

How certainly and securely he has left all behind in the grave which he took on himself on their behalf. In his death, in his burial, here is the twofold testimony: he has succeeded with divine success, and is the victor with superlative victory. Behold and see! Look into the tomb and tell if it be not so.

Here is a sure foundation for the resurrection and the world to come: it is Jesus Christ and him crucified.

Christ met the need of sinners where they stood, whilst they were still sinning. They were, moreover, oblivious of the grace of God being extended to secure a firm basis for his everlasting love thereafter to draw and thereupon to establish them. 'Jesus Christ and him crucified.' But whilst God was laying the foundation, they went on unknowing, unheeding; they sinned on uncaring.

Yet when called by grace, through the voice of the Son of God sounding in their hearts, they found that whilst they were in their iniquity and rebellion *God had done all that was needful in Christ already to procure their eternal salvation and endurance in the faith.*

Now then, who shall lay any charge to God's elect? He cannot get it *past the grave.* That took in everything, including the foreseen weakness and infirmity of a people not having strength from themselves to hold on their way to the end. Death answers even that, and life assures grace to do what man cannot. That is the nature of grace.

It is GOD that justifieth. And, whom he justified, them he glorified. There can be no question of his — his — ability to bring in those for whom Christ died. And were there, it would have been answered at the cross and confirmed in the grave. We see that. All questions answered.

Yet still a body to sigh in, and a groaning creation with which to share in travail. However, sighs, groans or not, there can be no doubt at all of the manifestation of the sons of God in the day that the glory comes and the crying ends.

That is grace; with Christ, risen, answering every need from the past, at the present and in the future, of absolute certainty. Witness the cross and the grave. A stable basis for an everlasting foundation from which there can be no departure and no erosion. None at all. Since departure and erosion were encountered there themselves, thence to be brought down to death and the tomb entirely to the divine satisfaction.

That is grace. He will bring his called, he will bring his elect, he will bring believers through to the end.

A Question

Abundant grace seen in the Epistle to the Ephesians shows the saints already — now — seated in glory. They do not wait till the end, and why should they, seeing what GOD hath wrought?

In Ephesians God looks on man as to nature and views him as completely dead, judged already, and the whole world as it were concluded in the grave. But in Christ, God and the Father views a people as if already raised from the dead by grace, and more also, seen as ascended with him and even now seated in heaven, alive and incorruptible in glory.

The Epistle to the Romans, however, takes a different view.

Man is seen as under responsibility to God. There is obligation by nature. In consequence, enlightened man looks up to God and, trembling, finds himself alive and accountable, hasting to the day of reckoning.

However, in the gospel, grace intervenes through Jesus Christ. In Christ the faithful see all their responsibility met, the debt paid, the account cancelled, and as to all that could call or recall his sanctified people to the strict justice of the judgment day: for ever dead with Christ and buried withal.

Then here all is grace and goodness come out from God, not regarding the deserts, merits, works or earnings of sinful men. Not imputing their trespasses unto them, but manifesting the grace of a Saviour God, setting Christ before all peoples, calling,

> Look unto me and be ye saved,
> all the ends of the earth.

for Pope John Paul II

And again, entreating by Jesus Christ,

> Earth, earth, earth,
> hear the word of the Lord.

The compassions of a God, the mercies of a Saviour, are displayed abundantly in the person of Jesus Christ, the beginning of the gospel of God, who was sent, and is come, without man's seeking or even his knowing.

None of the Jews could answer the question, 'Where is he that is born King of the Jews?' They had no idea where he was, nor who he is.

And no more has Christendom today.

But this sullen churlishness did not, and does not, deter God. Neither does the gross darkness that covers the people, nor yet the veil upon the face of all nations. He still sends Jesus Christ the light of the world, the beginning of the gospel of God, the Saviour, the Son of God. And he still sends his servants to preach Christ in the world.

The tragedy is that such grace, exterior to man, though set before his very eyes and sounding clearly in his ears, but brings out man for what he is within: fallen, dark and dead, at enmity against the God of light and life.

Nevertheless the gospel did not come to condemn men, or come to be a savour of death unto death unto them. It was sent to save men, to bring a sweet savour of Christ, to be a savour of life unto life, to bring salvation, to give grace and glory by Jesus Christ. It is Christ that is announced. God gives his Son for the life of the world. It is God's gospel.

Yet the answer to the gospel is from within. With the heart man believeth. And it is so that the secrets of many hearts may be made manifest.

Now God brings to light a hidden, well hidden, otherwise unknown treasure, sunk beneath and within the earth of this world. And whilst the gospel falls superficial and indifferent upon the earthen and earthy state of nature, God's hid treasure comes to light by the interior call of Christ quickening into life and awakening into faith.

This call from the voice of the Son of God is individual and personal. Alarmed by it, the heart cries, I have no righteousness!

But if it be a question of righteousness, it was known that man had none before the call came. And known that man cannot have to do with God without righteousness. Hence in Romans is manifested the righteousness of God for faith. The pathetic state of the unrighteous sinner, condemned under guilt and wrath, was all known to God before the call came. Hence, what the call brings is God's answer to that pathetic condition.

The gospel presents to the trembling gaze of the awakened sinner the one answer he could never think possible: that God had *a substitute instead of him,* who should and would take his case upon himself and resolve every question on the sinner's behalf. That is what the gospel reveals to lost sinners: another man than themselves, who has answered to God, to justice and to righteousness on their behalf and in their place. A substitutionary sacrifice in the sinner's place. *Another man to die on one's behalf:* Christ Jesus is his name; this dying substitute is the answer of God to the need of the sinner.

for Pope John Paul II

It is he to whom we are called, by whom we are called, and in whom we have been called to believe.

He is preached on in the world. And that reveals the loveless, graceless, dark, dead and earthen state of the world and worldly religion. A worldly religion which, whilst professing much of these things, denies the life and power and inward presence of the Saviour described, utterly confounding the real nature of spiritual things with carnal inventions and alternatives.

Nevertheless to the hearts of his own, his foreknown people, the secret is whispered, the voice sounds in an inward way, and through this interior call Jesus Christ calls the lost to himself, and henceforth they are called lost no longer. No longer. Beloved of God, even at Rome, they are called saints. And that marks them: saintliness, or, as we say, sanctification.

Now therefore the sum of the doctrine is this: having revealed the righteous wrath of God that man has brought upon himself in consequence of his rebellion and hypocrisy, the love of God for fallen man is made known in salvation. This salvation of God is exclusively confined to Jesus Christ, freely brings righteousness without works for faith, and is declared first in terms of his person and then in terms of his work.

Son of God and seed of David, the Lord Jesus Christ is set forth in the Epistle to the Romans from another view than that of the lowly humiliation in which he had been seen in the gospels.

There, he had been seen after the flesh, sent to the Jews alone. Here, he is seen no longer after the flesh. He is seen by the Spirit proclaiming salvation among all nations.

In the gospels, until the end, his work on earth was unfinished; Jesus was not yet glorified, nor the Spirit given. In the epistles, his work on earth had been concluded, he had been crucified, dead and buried. God had raised him from the dead and given him glory. Ascended into heaven, the Holy Ghost poured forth on earth, Jesus had been named both Lord and Christ, and declared in his true name and nature as Son, having been glorified. That is the position from which the epistles open. And from which Christ preaches within by the Holy Ghost from heaven. Now therefore from the glory his glory is inwardly manifested by the Spirit of truth. Into this life and power all his own are gathered from out of the world, and separated to be indwelt by one Spirit in one body here below.

The eleven apostles had seen Jesus ascending out of their sight being received up in the cloud. That cloud obscured their view into heaven. Nevertheless through it, Jesus passed.

However, the day of Pentecost being fully come, the Holy Ghost was given. Jesus was glorified, and had received and sent the promise of the Father in behalf of all whom he had purchased in his travail on earth. The clouds passed over, the shadows flew away, and in a few chapters Stephen, at the threshold of martyrdom, saw heaven open and the Son of man standing at the right hand of God. This vision, and the inward Spirit and power by which Stephen gave utterance to it, the Jews denied and blasphemed, raining stones upon the dying martyr who prayed for their forgiveness.

However, Paul's visions and revelations of glory surpassed

all that had gone before. Paul was caught up to the third heaven, in such an ecstasy that he could not tell whether in or out of the body. In paradise he heard things not lawful for a man to utter.

His vision, I say, surpassed all other: he saw the full revelation of grace and of glory. He saw into the very essence of things spiritual and divine. The light, life, love, everlasting power and heavenly glory of God appeared to him, and appeared in a way that transcended every previous revelation.

And this is what he saw as the gospel. This very vision was his gospel. Not the Son of man but the Son of God. Not the Son of man standing but the Son of God seated. Not the Son of man standing at the right hand of God but the Son of God seated on the throne of his Father. Not obscured by clouds, or opened in heaven to his view on earth, but as the body of heaven for clearness, as caught up to the place itself, seeing all unclouded, himself ascended into that very element and environment.

Oh, that is gospel revelation indeed!

Paul received the ultimate vision of glory. Not with further revelation yet to come, but with all that was to be given fully revealed, fully unveiled, so that the entire new testament unfolded to his view. Not to see the Son of man standing — as if poised for movement yet to take place — but the Son of the Father seated, the thing settled, at rest in the glory, tranquil in the righteousness of God.

This is what he saw. But he saw it as a situation of glory for the Son of God not on his own behalf alone, but for his people also. So effective had been his death, that

— evidently — the Son had carried with him into that most blessed, most restful place, all for whom he died. So much so, that when Paul sees the seated Son, he sees the saints at rest with him, seated in the same heavenly places in Christ.

Then what a death was that, which elevates those once so far off into the very presence of God in sonship.

What a death!

And Romans tells us exactly what manner of death he died, for whom he died, and what its effects precisely, setting before the believer the glorious person of the ascended Son of God.

The Lord Jesus Christ, the Son of God and seed of David. The Son of God! A divine person possessing divine nature, one in deity with the Father and with the Holy Ghost, one God, blessed for evermore, Amen.

He is divine, the true God and everlasting life, that eternal life which was with the Father — eternal Son — yet in the fulness of time come 'of the seed of David according to the flesh'. A body had been prepared him, the power of the Highest overshadowing the creation of this unique manhood. A true human body and real human nature are his, who 'came of the seed of David according to the flesh'.

Therefore this divine person, eternally possessed of the divine nature, by incarnation united that created human nature with his uncreated divine nature into the uniqueness of his own person. Son of God! The perfection of that body, of that peerless humanity, conceived of the virgin Mary by the Holy Ghost, now united and belonging to the deity of the eternal Son of God: oh, mystery sublime!

for Pope John Paul II

This is that manhood, this the humanity, which was brought down into death — yea, all God's floods and billows passed over him — into such a death, even the death of the cross, the death of sacrificial atonement, the death of substitutionary sacrifice made once and for all.

This is the one whom Paul saw — and the mystery of whose being and nature he discerned — in the visions of God, seated in glory. And Paul perceived that all must come from him, and from him alone, and from him in that very place of revelation from which the gospel speaks in blessing to men.

That gospel speaks, however — first of all — to men as they are in fact, not as they imagine themselves to be: rather as they are discovered to be by the judgment of God. And where is this? Responsible, under obligation and accountable. Man is found utterly guilty. Men are discovered transgressors of the law, fallen and condemned already, and under sentence of eternal wrath. 'The wrath of God abideth' on them.

But this once admitted from real heart experience, from the truth of it sunk into the inward parts, forthwith God speaks peace by Jesus Christ, speaking peace by his sacrifice. He commands the faith of the broken and contrite in heart to rest in confidence in Jesus' blood shed and person raised in their behalf. And to establish that confidence, in Romans they are to see themselves dead in his death, and view themselves buried in his grave.

We are to have total and absolute confidence that we may rest in him. We have peace with God who repose upon him, because that, seated in heaven, he rests in God, and God rests in him, and both in respect of the people whom

75

he ransomed in death. This is the man Christ Jesus whom the gospel presents to faith, declaring that God will not only accept but has accepted, and more than accepted, he had before appointed that man to take our cause in hand on earth. This cause he took up. He will not lay it down nor leave it until, victorious in death, he is raised from the dead, thereafter with triumph to appear in heaven ever to make intercession for us.

And if so, then who can be against us?

For a man is seen in heaven by the gospel.

He is not the first man Adam, who was seen on earth by the creation. Wrath is revealed from heaven against that man of sin and death, and to all his earthly offspring.

But the gospel declares another man, a second man, the last Adam, the Lord from heaven, a man with five scars now glorified, righteousness of God his own element and his right on his saints' behalf. This is the Son of God in glory. This is manhood in glory. And faith is to see herself in this man who acted as surety on her behalf, see herself seated in the Son of God in glory. And if so, first having died in him and with him and buried withal.

This is the doctrine conveyed to faith in the Epistle to the Romans, as it regards the person of Christ.

Finally there is the work of Christ.

This work is the righteousness of God wrought in death by the faith of Jesus Christ, unto all and upon all them that believe.

The work of righteousness is a work wrought in death, precisely that of which man stands in such desperate want. The death of Christ answers to the appalling need of man in two aspects. It meets,

1st. The righteousness of the law, that is, the righteousness of human nature, human rectitude, required of man in and of himself.

2nd. The righteousness of God, that is, the righteousness of God's nature, divine righteousness, proper to God in and of himself.

If God is to dwell with men, these two righteous requirements must be satisfied in all justice.

All righteousness must be fulfilled.

It is one thing for the broken law to be vindicated, the law of God to be justified, so that law is requited and justice done in respect of law-breaking man.

But it is quite another thing to ascend above all that is created, to penetrate the heavenly places themselves above all heavens, there to approach the light unapproachable, which no man hath seen nor can see: then what glory is this? That of righteousness proper and intrinsic to the divine being.

What the gospel tells us is that the blood of Christ answers to both these needs for guilty sinners, withal to justify them freely by grace, and bring them to God and God to them.

A Question

'Behold,
the tabernacle of God is with men,
and he will dwell with them,
and they shall be his people,
and God himself shall be with them,
and be their God.'

Then, all righteousness fulfilled.

Until man is reckoned to have such a righteousness to perfection, he must be expelled for ever even from the uttermost reaches of the presence of God. And this, no matter what might come to man on earth by the law, though it were through Christ and his death.

Two things are certain of the righteousness of God if God and men are to dwell together: God shall have it and man has not got it. And quite apart from the broken law, that also is the divine, the gospel, the sublime reason for the blood of Christ. It was why that blood was shed. Not only to meet the curse of the law but to answer to God's own nature in righteousness.

When the poor, the mourning, the meek, when they who hunger and thirst after righteousness fix their eyes by faith upon that blood, God reckons what that blood achieved to the account of those believers. He puts righteousness to the sinner's account.

God's righteous judgment was the cause of the blood being shed, and if so, then of that judgment being satisfied. Thus justice and judgment are reconciled in righteousness. For sinners. He died for sinners. That reconciliation was for sinners.

When the man that believes fastens his faith on the

blood shed on his behalf, his faith is reckoned to him for righteousness. Not that he has done anything to work it nor to fetch it, but what he sees and believes is this: by Jesus Christ, God has done it all.

Then the blood of Christ equals the demands of all righteousness against the sinner. Then, through that blood applied, all righteousness, now satisfied, is put to the account of faith.

> 'Faith is reckoned to him
> for righteousness.'

And, I say, it is not only the righteousness of a full discharge from law, but the divine righteousness of the everlasting God. Then, the penitent hath that wherewith to answer to his presence, and by it appear before God, and God appear to him. He may answer to him with whom we have to do. And so it proves in experience.

But is this too much? Shall man then be just with God? Is it so in reality? In experience? Is it possible for men actually to enter and be at peace in the very presence of God? Can it be?

No, never, until and unless righteousness is satisfied in all its aspects. For naturally, a vehement and infinite controversy rages against man in behalf of everlasting righteousness outraged in every way, and outraged absolutely.

But what faith sees in the Son of God is a saviour other than oneself. Faith sees a manhood other than that of fallen humanity. A man distinct from oneself: yet in fact acting instead and in place of self. Appointed by God to do so, on behalf of all those beloved of God and called saints.

And what does one see? One sees the man Christ Jesus

sitting at rest in heaven, at repose, ascended, entered and at rest in the very presence of God, in the very throne of the Father himself.

But, cries the soul, what of me? That I believe of him; but what of myself?

Consider. Consider that the Son of God, he in whom manhood is exalted to glory, is in that manhood exalted and scarred. Here is a man whose scars proclaim in glory, in heaven now, that once on earth, in a suffering sacrifice for sinners, all righteousness was fulfilled. That every righteous demand was met and all justice fully requited. Then for whom? For whoever, those glorified scars proclaim their acceptance with God! They declare that the once suffering, now glorified Saviour:

1st. Paid the price of man's unrighteousness, when he endured the curse of the law. 'Cursed is every one that hangeth on a tree.' Then 'Christ hath redeemed us from the curse of the law, being made a curse for us,' and furthermore by his death we 'are not under the law'.

2nd. Reached in his sufferings even to those stupendous heavenly heights of the righteousness of God. He answered to all that was required by the essential being of God from guilty sinners, to bring them even into his everlasting glory and presence and unto the divine nature. Witness the ascended, seated, glorified Son, now and for ever bearing the scars of his work to bring them where he is, that there they may be also.

Had the Saviour not paid this untold price, he would not, and he could not, now rest in the presence of God in the glory. Nor could the visible testimony of what he undertook — to bring sinners to God — rest there with him. But his scars are there, they do rest there, and they are with him always. And he is resting in the presence of God in the glory. And that rest itself proclaims the perfection and the perfect satisfaction of the work he did on earth, for all those for whom it was done.

This work — factually reported in the four gospels, spiritually expounded in the several epistles — was prefigured under the old testament. 'Being witnessed by the law and the prophets.'

In the courtyard outside the house of God — or temple — stood the brazen altar. This was a clear figure of the cross of Calvary, the place of sacrifice on earth. The sacrifices of beasts, such as lambs, we are told, typified the forthcoming offering up of Jesus outside Jerusalem.

When that time came, this was the place — outside the camp — that Christ was offered up a sacrifice for sin. Bearing the transgressions of his people, he died to make atonement for sins. That is, for all the guiltworthy rebellion exposed in the first three chapters of Romans, and all the corrupt and offensive state of the flesh revealed in chapters five to seven. Christ bare it all away once for all in his sacrifice upon the accursed tree. This substitutionary offering cancelled all the debt by blood, even the blood of the everlasting covenant.

All this was foreshadowed in the figures of old time in Israel. They were pictures of the reality which was one day to take place in Christ.

A Question

The enactment of just such a figure is seen when Aaron, the high priest under the old testament, took some of this blood of sacrifice shed at the brazen altar — figuratively Calvary — and carried it within the house of God, the temple, into the Holy Place.

On this singular occasion he was permitted and required to penetrate even to the sanctuary, the Holiest of All. Only once a year he entered this inmost temple. This was on the annual 'day of atonement', Yom Kippur.

The high priest then entered, with clouds of incense, and, trembling, passed through the unrent veil into the most holy presence of God. Fearfully he sprinkled ahead of him with the same blood that had been shed far outside, previously spilt on the earth, poured out in the courtyard at the side of the altar of sacrifice. Aaron took this blood as he passed into the Holiest to stand before the very presence of God. Wreathed in incense, he appeared with fear and trembling to face the mercy seat or propitiatory itself, overshadowed on either side by the golden cherubim of glory. Seven times with his finger he sprinkled upon that golden propitiatory, the tremendous sense of ALMIGHTY GOD striking awe to his very heart.

Nevertheless thus, and only thus, was atonement — not rendered but — prefigured under the old testament. Though the sacrifice of atonement was made without, on 'Yom Kippur', the blood of atonement must appear within.

Now, on the one hand, it is quite clear that the place without, the brazen altar, prefigured the cross of Calvary.

But, on the other hand, the Holiest of All within the temple depicted another scene entirely. Here was prefigured a temple made without hands, a holy place high in the heavens, the very dwelling place of the God of glory in the highest. And the golden mercy seat or propitiatory upon which the high priest at last sprinkled the blood taken within, this also typified another place altogether. That is, typified it under the old testament, for the time then present. The 'mercy seat' signified another place than ever appeared on earth, or was to be found in this present world below.

So then, the figure of the blood-sprinkled mercy seat within the temple is far different from the picture of the blood shed at the brazen altar in the courtyard outside. That is, it is no longer the sacrifice outside before man on earth, seen to meet man's debts by the offering up of the substitute at Calvary. For now that blood of the covenant is viewed as taken inside. It is within the sanctuary, before God, taken into his holy temple, inside the house of God, into the Holiest of All. Within the veil.

And where is this? This typifies the blood of the covenant, shed on earth, taken up into the highest. By Jesus Christ, our priest and mediator, taken to appear before God in heaven itself.

'Christ being come an high priest of good things to come,
by a greater and more perfect tabernacle,
not made with hands.'
Hebrews 9:11.

'For Christ is not entered into the holy places
made with hands,
which are the figures of the true;
but into heaven itself,
now to appear in the presence of God for us.'
Hebrews 9:24.

On the day of atonement the high priest passed within the old testament sanctuary, entering within the veil, there to appear before the very presence of Jehovah. For now it is a question of propitiating Jehovah himself in his own person. No longer a question of God approving the sacrifice outside, meeting the shortcomings of human righteousness according to the law. Here in the Holiest of All it is a matter of the demands of the nature of God, of the divine righteousness. Here, at the golden 'mercy seat', God himself in his own being is to be rendered propitious by the blood of atonement.

So Christ, having died on earth, ascended into heaven itself there to present the perfection of that work below which not only met the curse of the law on earth, but actually glorified God in his nature in heaven.

The virtue of his blood; the testimony of his five scars; his appearance in the house not made with hands, higher than the heavens; his being received up into glory; and above everything else, his reigning in triumph from his Father's throne: all these things bear witness to that wonderful Saviour, and the perfect work of the Lord Jesus Christ.

This was the answering reality, no longer the prefiguring shadow. The substance had come, no longer to be witnessed by feeble type and picture. At last appeared in spiritual reality the divine answer to the ancient question:

How shall man be just with God?

Not by the figures under the old covenant but by the truth under the new: by the work of Jesus Christ in death, attested by the answering glory of heaven.

84

Hence I conclude that herein lies the understanding of the doctrine in Romans. Which is the same thing as the beginning of the gospel. It is to see that when guilty man is brought to account before God, and the wrath of God is revealed against all his ungodliness and unrighteousness, God provides an answer.

An answer that men think they understand, but few really understand by revelation and experimentally. Hence what they do instead is to repeat old formulae, dead men's creeds, reiterating like schoolchildren the stultified thoughts of brains long turned to dust. No freshness, no life, no power, no love: nothing for or from themselves out of heaven! No immediate experience of the light of Christ.

But God's answer to guilty men who feel their lost estate under the wrath of God is to bring to light in the gospel, before the eye of faith, *another man altogether.* Another man appears!

The first man, of the earth, earthy, was made a living soul. He is seen as the one who was from below, who fell, who brought in sin and death. This is the one in whom we are born of our natural parents, and, as responsible, find our account in dreadful arrears and ourselves without hope of paying the debt.

But the second man is the Lord from heaven; he is revealed as that life-giving Spirit, the last Adam, the Saviour from above.

He comes through the grace of God freely bestowing righteousness and life by sheer mercy to all the chosen seed, all who in Christ are born of God and quickened by his word. He declares the faith of the gospel, that he has paid the account of those with nothing to pay, blotting out their debt by the shedding of his own blood at Calvary. He appears, I say, in interior soul-transforming light and power.

Here is the heart of Romans; here is the revelation of the mystery: what God now reveals completely transcends the one man, Adam, together with his posterity, born of and continuing in his image and destined for this present world. But with a destiny for the world to come, the gospel has brought to light another man, a second man, a last Adam, with an entirely distinct, interior and spiritual posterity, now begotten by him out of heaven.

Yet the worldly church, traditional Christendom, is convinced to the contrary. And in its dreams and suppositions, the present age naturally cannot imagine a Christ other than one centred upon itself, its passing world and its own destiny. A Christ come in a haphazard general sort of way to try to do his best for the world and patch it up, if possible blessing here and there. To help whom he may, or, at least, whoever might be of the type inclined to be helped. Or, pitying his apparently pathetic stance, might let him help.

What an utter travesty of both Christ and the gospel!

But, oh, that men would grasp this: there is another man than nature conceives or this world dreams of, with another — a spiritual — posterity begotten by him and after his own image, nothing to do with the first.

This second man begets and shall beget, but not as did the first man of the earth by carnal seed. The second man is the Lord from heaven who begets with that spiritual seed, by regeneration in the Holy Ghost, through the word of God. After his own image he begets, heavenly and spiritual, and shall yet beget when he raises his own from the dead.

Then, risen, they who have been in this life born of and spiritually conformed to him within, really, truly and powerfully sanctified and made perfect in love, these shall rise immortal. They shall be conformed to him even in the body of glory:

> 'We shall be like him;
> for we shall see him as he is.'

Yet now, at present, his chosen seed are manifest:

> 'As he is,
> so are we in this world.'

Not one kind exists, then, but two kinds of men, the second chosen out and having life from Christ.

But if such a distinction, why are they not more manifest?

> 'Therefore the world knoweth us not,
> because it knew him not.'

They, the world, the religious world into which he came, as well as the world outside it, never knew that he was another creation than themselves. Never knew that he would inwardly beget after his own image by the Holy Ghost, by the word of God, to create a new man after his own image. The world does not know.

And, today, since you never preached it, they are even less likely to know now. But it is still true.

There is a certain analogy with his birth true to that of

his own people. His manhood came by the power of God, by the Holy Ghost, by the overshadowing of the Almighty. And, within, by the Spirit, drawn by the Father, his own are born anew in that interior light, life and power of the Son of God, the life-giving Spirit, the second man from heaven.

He has appeared in the gospel.

Not by any means to put new wine into old bottles. Not to leave believers under the genealogy of the man in whom they were naturally begotten, of whom they were born by nature. Not to leave them trembling under conviction of sin and unbelief in Adam, in whom they would await a certain and a fearful judgment, to know no rest but only everlasting torment in outer darkness from the presence of the Lord.

But Christ has appeared, having died on earth and cancelled every debt by his death below. He appears and begets souls to himself by his radiant light and quickening word through the gospel, God reckoning an entirely new genealogy in him. Sons of God!

Behold,
what manner of love the Father hath bestowed upon us,
that we should be called the children of God!

Truly, the new wine is for new bottles.

Now, today, Christ comes by the Spirit, preaching everlasting righteousness freely reckoned for faith in his blood. Eternal life he freely bestows by the gift of God, abundantly flowing in the springing well of the Holy Ghost in the inward parts. The Son of God baptises all those for whom he died on earth with the Holy Ghost from heaven above.

So that notwithstanding the state of man on earth, the fearful, the hopeless condition of the world, the very soon-coming end of time: I say, notwithstanding, there is another man in glory, sitting at rest in the presence of God.

Here is one who knows his own in the world, even unto this present, and is ready to hear the crying of the oppressed and the sighing of the needy once more. This is the one who will return with great power and glory, to change, raise and gather all his saints out of every kindred and tongue and people and nation, from all generations, in the resurrection of the just, world without end, Amen. This is that Son of God. Christ Jesus is his name. He is the man Christ Jesus, the one mediator between God and men.

Glory be to God. Amen.

On high he bears five scars.

Four were incurred whilst he was alive. The outrage of these wounds occurred when they nailed his hands and his feet to the tree. When, lifted up, he began the long hours of his travail as the vicarious sacrifice for sin and as the substitute for sinners.

But the fifth scar marked that this work was already finished; it testified that his travail was ended. For the last scar was inflicted when all was over. He was dead already when the lance pierced his side. His suffering and anguished passion had been completed between four scars and five. Between life and in death. With the fifth his blood was shed, and water withal. Then blood is mentioned — not without water — and not till then, only then, when he was dead already. Only John records it. Only the spiritual perceive it. 'And the living, the living, he shall praise thee, as I do this day.' The living shall declare the mystery of the faith. Yet who does so?

Did you, Sir?

Were I to ask you questions on this, out of John, the meaning of this mystery — you who with me share this name of John — could you answer? You know whether you could answer. And so do I.

But God raised him from the dead. He ascended on high. God gave him glory. He is seated on the throne of his Father. Now it no longer follows that man shall never rest in the presence of God. Behold the Man! God elevated him to the throne of glory where he sits and reigns tranquil. At rest in light unapproachable, at peace in the righteousness of God.

This shows how completely, how perfectly, he obtained justification for the ungodly through his work on behalf of sinners here on earth. Because he had identified himself with them at Calvary, having taken their entire and dreadful state upon himself, it follows that he could not thereafter sit in glory on their behalf *had he not atoned to perfection for all that stood between them and the glory where now he rests.*

He answered completely all the failure of the sinner here below. He took upon himself the punishment due to men for lack of righteousness — all ungodliness and all unrighteousness — as it appeared before the brazen altar in the ancient figure. That is Calvary, the altar; and he who hung there suspended is the Lamb of God, the sacrifice. He is the sinbearer for sinful men, the substitutionary atonement of sinners, the reconciliation.

Thenceforth and thereafter, by resurrection and in ascension, he took the priceless value of his shed blood into heaven. He went 'within the veil'. A cloud received him out of their sight. Veiled him from them. In heaven, out of sight, he appeared before the propitiatory mercy seat of the righteousness of God in glory.

There he was to sprinkle, in a figure to sprinkle, the heavenly propitiatory seven times to perfection in blood with his own finger. Drop by drop. Not as a flood when shed on earth, the outpouring of blood urgent before the impending wrath and outrage from heaven. But now, in heaven, sprinkled with precision, drop by drop; so particular; what is priceless exposed to view. That which purchases his own, known by name, carefully displayed before the very righteousness of God.

So he appeared and so he sprinkled.

> 'Whom God hath set forth a propitiation
> through faith in his blood.'

The law, silenced and satisfied, no longer in view, for ever sealed within the ark. Nor can it, nor shall it, ever be seen again. Not there, not beyond death and the grave. Not in the glory. Nor to a people glorified. Christ is their all in all.

The message of grace to faith peals forth from heaven:

> 'Believe on the Lord Jesus Christ,
> and thou shalt be saved, and thy house.'

91

A Question

Christ appears for the faithful in glory. Yet in a mystery he speaks the sinner on earth into faith from that glory. A second man, from whom now the faithful, the saints, are to count their birth and draw all their life. The Lord from heaven, he whose inheritance by the resurrection from the dead is that of the coming glory. He rests in the presence of God for us, to appear for us, so that all he is on our behalf has been reckoned to our account. The Son of God, the Lord Jesus Christ.

He is the one to whom inwardly and experimentally the Holy Ghost unites us, in the interior man. He is the one in whom we live and stand. This is he in whom God counts our new existence: another existence, another inheritance, in another man entirely, in the Saviour by the grace of God.

Now then, this is he who by faith is grasped and held in the gospel.

And in principle, this is the sum, the concept, the essence of the revelation in the doctrine of the Epistle to the Romans.

Now, I have delivered my soul in all honesty. May the Pope not mistake the plainness of speech demanded by clarity of conscience for any rude impertinence or coarse behaviour on my part. God forbid.

Before God, I lie not: I have declared what I believe I have received from the God of my salvation. What I received, that is, when, in my years of solitude, I looked for divine revelation on the evangelical Epistle to the Romans.

Nor would I have gone so far as to write and publish this book, had I not been as certain of the leading of God to do so, as I was certain then of being led in those years to seek the Lord that I might be taught of him alone. Which things I believe to be right before God and honouring to Christ. 'I believed; therefore have I spoken.' But not lightly, nor easily.

This summarises what I believe I received as on my knees out of my spiritual anguish in the solitary places. What I believe I was taught in the teaching of the Holy Ghost in answer to many prayers and cries over many years. What I believe came to me in much chastening, much humiliation, much brokenness of heart, in much spiritual exercise to know both the word and power of the apostle in the gospel.

Sir, after this, how can I not speak plainly?

The stock of the English, that people from whom I come, are plain, blunt, honest and straightforward men: but when above all nature the baptism of the Holy Ghost fills a man, and the prophetic fire kindles within him, burning in the very bones, what will ye?

Sound speech, plainly delivered, is demanded, not to be condemned.

Now then, I say that the doctrine I have delivered is the sum of the doctrine that went to Rome in the apostle's time.

It was not about politics, humanitarian or social problems, the present life or world, worldly advice or the aspiration of growing youth, no, not at all. However prudent, sage or witty your speech on such things, it was not what the apostle sent to Rome. Nor does his doctrine concern efforts for alleviation of earthly poverty, distribution of wealth, inequality, sickness, human woe or earthly unhappiness. Though no doubt individually, privately and unseen, these things would follow the gospel in consequence as circumstances permitted.

But these things are not the gospel, nor the direct concern of the gospel.

Rather, if we are poor, the gospel teaches us to endure and suffer such things as submitting to the providence of God and looking for the return of the Lord.

And, if rich, to sell what we have and give to the poor, and come, follow him.

But the doctrine, the apostolic doctrine, is about SALVATION. From the wrath to come. For ever. In the world to come. After death. It is about the power of God unto *salvation*, this gospel of Christ, of which Paul was not ashamed. And it is the power of God unto salvation, because therein is the righteousness of God revealed from faith to faith, as it is written, The just shall live by faith.

It is about salvation. Timeless problems of sin and judgment; of immortality; of eternity; of heaven and hell: how to be saved from such massive, overwhelming, agonising and all-absorbing problems.

From which any worldly focus, especially on the alleviation of earthly problems, dulls and deadens the soul.

'Hath not God chosen the poor of this world rich in faith?'

94

Not rich in socio-political redistributions. Welfare systems having nothing but the cynical selfishness of politicians as their motive. And how could a righteous God bless that?

He blesses the poor because they are poor, not out of poverty but in it. Their very poverty becomes their blessing. Have you never read the rich man and Lazarus? This world is nothing: the world to come everlasting.

Salvation!

How to find it? Where may it be found? Here is the place where the Lord tarries: in the gospel. Here he is known and met in the aching heart, at the place of faith. The epistle declares it, and that by divine revelation. This is the antidote to the prince of darkness. It is eyesalve for the blindness of the soul to the light from heaven. It is 'Ephphatha' to the interior deafness of the heart to the Spirit's voice within. The gospel is health for sickness of soul.

It is the only knowledge of God; it is the power of God; it brings the light, life and love that he is: this is the gospel, and it is received by soul-melting evangelical faith and heart-broken spiritual repentance alone.

Though many, multitudes, who think themselves evangelical have no such experience: only the dead letter. Mere exterior text. Or overheated feeling and imagination. Nothing but the outward description of what they have never felt within: and they call this faith!

But not to stop with them. For I am to appeal to you, Pope John Paul II. To you, because of these things you did not speak.

A Question

The apostolate you claim for your authority wrote this scripture for Rome and taught this doctrine to Rome in order that from Rome might be published abroad the salvation of God. Published abroad, that is, to the immortal souls of perishing sinners in a lost world, by faith in Christ only.

Of this gospel Paul was not ashamed.

The papacy speaks from Rome and appeals for authority to the scriptures. Very well then, and what scripture more appropriate than that which came to Rome? What? What! Saith he,

> 'What?
> came the word of God out from you?
> or came it unto you only?'

Let that therefore sound from you, which in truth came unto you. For you appeal to scripture, and — so far as I can see — not the scripture, anywhere, much less the relevant scripture to Rome — to which I have appealed — bears the least resemblance whatsoever to your speeches.

What the Pope says in the world and to the world, appears to me as of the world, worldly. At least, so it appears from scripture.

For this you will never suffer persecution for the cross of Christ. But Peter did, Paul did, the true minister must, I certainly do, and by the time you and yours have finished with me, probably will much more, because the gospel brings it invariably.

So that of the gospel of which the apostle Paul was not ashamed, Pope John Paul II appears ashamed, preferring popular humanitarianism, moral generalities and social alleviations.

And the sum and the substance of my question is this: WHY ON EARTH APPEAL FROM THAT TO THE SCRIPTURES?

Unless, of course, I have deceived myself?

For I know that the heart is deceitful above all things and desperately wicked; who can know it? O cleanse thou me from secret faults; keep back thy servant also from presumptuous sins. I know that none were more blind than those religious who said, 'I see.' I know that to be stiffnecked, uncircumcised in heart and ears, to be swollen with the leaven of the Pharisees, quite blinds the eyes to the truth about oneself, and the truth in itself.

Yet I know in my heart and conscience that I have judged myself. I know that in the light of Christ I have been brought off the fleshly mind, off self-confidence, to cry and pray and wait long in dependence upon him, upon the moving of the Spirit, and to try this by the word of God and test it with the passage of time. I know I have applied the scripture, 'If in any thing ye be otherwise minded, God shall reveal even this unto you.'

It would be nothing but false witness to deny that witness of the Spirit in which I am sure within myself that I have received of the Lord both the teaching of Romans and the inspiration for this book.

I know by years of trial, of tribulation, of waiting, that I received my ministry neither of men nor by man; nor do I have to appeal to men to support it, nor will I constantly quote others to justify myself as though I am unsure of my position. But I have appealed to the scripture, to the sole authority, to the most pertinent scripture, to the Epistle to the Romans itself.

Besides, to appeal to the scripture is just what you have done. But I cannot see how this possibly justifies you, and hence I ask my question.

Unless that be wrong? Unless you judge yourself above being questioned? Do you do that?

If you do that, if you deny me or anyone else the right to question you, then you put yourself above the Lord Jesus, who answered every question; in the gospels it may be seen clearly. Likewise if you deny me or anyone else the right to judge, and judge publicly, what you say, then you put yourself above the apostles, who said to the believers, 'Judge ye what I say.' How then can it be wrong to do so? Or I, how can I be wrong to follow this scripture, seeing you have appealed to scripture for authority?

I ask again, as to the substance of what I have set forth, for which I have been so many years in spiritual and solitary exercises: Is this of heaven or of man?

If of man, convince me of error from the same epistle. Or, since the epistle rises from the gospel foundations, then convince me by the same gospel. And convince me by more heavenliness not more worldliness; more gospel not more politics; more plain honesty not more Jesuitical subtlety; more spirituality not more humanism; more scripture not more tradition: convince me by a more correct conclusion. I will gladly bow.

But if what I have received, what I have set down, if it

be of God, I beg you to own it. I plead with you to lead us all aright in the word of truth, the gospel of our salvation. Because the apostles have taught us that in the belief of that gospel alone can be found the eternal safety and bliss of our immortal souls. Do this, Sir, I beg you, on my knees I beg you, and I for one will gladly follow, laying down my pen to write no more. Why then should I write more? For, in such a case, a better and more proper advocate would appear than so unfit and insignificant a person as myself.

But if you will not do it; if, with all your prominence, all your pre-eminent opportunities, with a world that listens as to an oracle, if you will not do it: of what enormities are you guilty?

And do you then expect the silence of heaven? Or the silence of his servants, who dwells in heaven? Or the silence of that long-absent spirit of prophecy from on high?

Yea, the very stones would cry out.

Moreover

> 'He that sitteth in the heavens shall laugh:
> the LORD shall have them in derision.
> Then shall he speak unto them in his wrath,
> and vex them in his sore displeasure.'

He shall speak, and who shall let it?

You may well say: 'Who do you think you are?' 'Who are you?'

And I have answered already: 'Nothing; less than nothing.'

A Question

You may reply: 'Then, Nothing, hold your peace against the Pope and all the world! Who are you that disturbs the peace? Who are you to find all of us at fault? Who are you that think everyone out of step but yourself?'

Sir, I am a lost sheep that went astray: but the Lord found me. I am one that destroyed my life: but the Lord saved it. I am one that sank to the depths and became altogether filthy: but the Lord drew me out of deep mire, out of the pit where there was no standing. He washed me; he set my feet on a rock; he put a new song in my mouth; he established my goings. Yea, he loved me and he does love me. I am nothing. Nothing but his. Nothing but his slave. Nothing but his servant, to speak his word at heaven's command.

As to your peace: saith my Master, I came not to bring peace but a sword.

As to my finding fault: God forbid; I am of myself nothing but fault. It is he that is faultless.

As to all men being in error: have you never heard this scripture:

'Yea, let God be true, but every man a liar' ?

> The Apostle Paul
> Epistle to the Romans ch. 3:4.

Or if, after all, you have a predilection for tradition over scripture, then have you never heard this proverb:

'Athanasius contra mundum' ?

INCREASED PRICES

When first the Trust was raised up, we printed and bound all our own books, passing on to the public little more than the cost of paper and ink. Freely we had received, freely we gave.

Now it has pleased God so to bless this work that no longer are we able to meet the demands for our books by the small and laborious hand-processing with which we began the work.

Therefore, having sold out of most of our stocks, we are obliged to fulfil present and future orders by having our books made by the up-to-date methods of professional printers elsewhere, and hence the considerable price rise.

Our principles however remain the same: not only are these reprinted titles passed on to the public at less than cost, but all of us at the Trust give you our services without money and without price. As always, there are no royalties or publisher's costs relayed to the public by the John Metcalfe Publishing Trust.

Why not? Because we seek our own benefit? God knoweth, we seek not our own, not yours but you, that you may be blessed from God the Father by Jesus Christ our Lord, in the free knowledge of the gospel of the grace of God.

'Thanks be unto God for his unspeakable gift.'

ORDER FORM

Quantity

Noah and the Flood . . . . £1.20 + *26p* ☐

Divine Footsteps . . . . 40p + *17p* ☐

The Red Heifer . . . . 75p + *21p* ☐

The Wells of Salvation . . . . £1.50 + *41p* ☐

Of God or Man? . . . . £1.45 + *36p* ☐

A Question for Pope John Paul II . . £1.25 + *26p* ☐

The Two Prayers of Elijah . . . . 10p + *10p* ☐

The Gospel of God . . . . 25p + *14p* ☐

The Strait Gate . . . . 25p + *14p* ☐

Eternal Sonship and Taylor Brethren . . 25p + *14p* ☐

Foundations Uncovered . . . . 30p + *17p* ☐

The Birth of Jesus Christ . . . . 95p + *26p* ☐

The Messiah . . . . £2.45 + *75p* ☐

The Son of God and Seed of David . £1.10 + *46p* ☐

(Figures in italics show postage costs for single copies, which are correct at time of going to press and apply to the U.K. only)

NAME AND ADDRESS (in block capitals)

—————————————————————————————————

—————————————————————————————————

—————————————————————————————————

Please enclose remittance with order.
Cheques and postal orders payable to 'The Publishing Trust'.

cut here